MW01519590

GOD SPEAKS HIS HEART

**A collection of messages
from Holy Spirit, Christ and
Archangel Raphael
1980-1995**

**Received by
Reverend H. R. McClellan**

GOD SPEAKS HIS HEART
A Spiritual Message

Published by:

Stuart Victor Publishing
Post Office Box 60322
Phoenix, Arizona 85082-0322. USA
e-mail   StuartVictor@inficad.com

All rights reserved USA and International. No part of this book
may be used or reproduced in any manner whatsoever without
written permission from the author except for brief quotations
or reviews.

Copyright 1996 by Helen R. McClellan
First Printing 1996
Printed in the United States of America

Cover Artwork by Arthur Douet from *Light of His
Countenance*

ISBN 0-9653155-3-3   Softcover
Library of Congress   96-61138

God Speaks His Heart - Holy Spirit & Archangel Raphael
1. Holy Spirit - New prophecies - miscellanea
2. Archangels - Raphael
3. Spiritual Dimension
4. Earth Changes

IN APPRECIATION

This book is dedicated with loving gratitude to the special people in my family who have always supported me with unconditional love.

My special thanks to Arthur Douet, a spiritually attuned artist, who drew upon his wonderful talents to re-create my vision of Archangel Raphael.

To the Holy Father and the Angels who have shown me the beauty of their love and helped me find the joy in my own life.

About the Author

I was born and grew up in England. In my early 20's, I felt a strong desire to travel and explore. After touring a few European countries I was motivated to leave England and settle in the U.S. Shortly after my arrival, I met and married a wonderful man who has been my life partner for the last 34 years.

Around 1980, I underwent a deep spiritual awakening which had a profound impact upon my perspectives. I started to experience life on a much deeper level.

My new journey soon enveloped me in friendships with many people of all ages and different races. With the help of the angels I endeavored to encourage people to discover their own spirit, and draw upon their inner beauty and strengths.

Recently I have found my path has changed again, since I am now devoting more of my time and energy to sharing the words I have received from the Holy One and the angels. The material for my next book "Children of the Earth Light" is still being received.

Reverend H. R. McClellan

"During the three years I have known Helen I have found her to be a sincere person always willing to help other people. She has an extraordinary ability to receive information from "higher sources" which I have always found to be of a positive spiritual and uplifting nature. She uses this ability to help others gain a deeper understanding of themselves. I feel that I have gained in spirituality, knowledge and wisdom in knowing Helen and I'm sure she will benefit others in the future."

John M. Lee, Doctor of Osteopathy

"I met Helen in the early 1990's when we found ourselves both serving Spirit together. I immediately realized something about her was unique. Her inner light shone through, she was always positive, and smiling. I realized she has such love for people in general. After reading her book I understand where she gets her spiritual strengths and insights. It was like going home again, back to our Father/Mother God, our Source. Thank you Helen, for sharing this valuable wisdom with us."

Reverend Judy E. Love

"Thank you. . . .for your prayers. Your kind words means a great deal to me, and I hope that you will continue to pray for peace and for God's blessings on our nation as we face the challenges ahead."

President George Bush, 1990

To Our Readers

This book has a very warm spiritual message, its call has gone out to the many who are open to receiving. I believe we have entered an era of Divine intervention, leading us into the remembrance of our spiritual roots.

There is nothing more precious or beautiful than to feel the Father's divine love flowing through our body, mind and spirit. It is with this thought in mind, that I pray to link God's heart with yours, in everlasting unity.

A limited amount of editing has been done to preserve the authenticity of the messages. The book was never intended to be a literary masterpiece, only a very simple message of love. Therefore I apologize for any errors which I may have overlooked.

Reverend H. R. McClellan

Contents

Contents

Forethoughts

For thousands of years humanity has been trying to connect to, or understand more about the Spirit of God, as well as our own spiritual nature. Various beliefs and interpretations have led us in many different directions. Most of us arrive at that basis which feels comfortable enough for us to pursue, and then we willingly follow those interpretations knowing it is the right path for us to take. If we look at the many religions, we will see that although each has a specific concept, **the end result is the same.** We all want to get to where God is.

The mystery of the roots of our existence and what life is all about is still in question. As we progress in our human intellect, we are learning to analyze and reason. In other words, our **awareness** factor is growing. The more we seek answers, the more we build upon what we have as our base. If we fail to question then we stagnate, since we are not growing toward our ultimate truth.

With the development of science, we have made many discoveries concerning our human origins, leading us to challenge the validity of our known beliefs. We have found ourself divided between what we have discovered as proof of our early human form, and our spiritual teachings. Slowly, we are discovering we are not one person, but two. A duality, representing an **outer** human form and an **inner** spirit.

What we regarded as truth eons ago, may not be the same truth that we recognize today. Our ever-inquiring mind still challenges us to search for answers. Gradually, we are beginning to fit all the smaller pieces together into one giant puzzle.

There must come a time in our history when the puzzle of our existence is finished, and then we can examine our past, present and future heritage, from what we have collectively concluded.

Introduction

I first sensed the presence of the angels in 1974. It was around the time we had a major fire in our house. It was quite an emotional setback for the family to realize we had lost just about everything we owned. Even our most precious possessions (early pictures of the baby, movies of our life, and other souvenirs) had all gone up in smoke. The only consolation to us was that no one was hurt.

We found that we had to move into a small apartment while our house was being rebuilt and it was during this time that I sensed an unusual Presence around me, giving me comfort and easing me through some very difficult months. I believed God was watching over us and I felt very grateful.

In 1980 I felt this very kind Presence around me again. This time, I heard a voice speaking to me through my thoughts. It was a male voice, young sounding, and very gentle. He identified himself as Raphael, a divine angel. He said he had been sent to the Earth for the purpose of healing and preparation for the return of the Divine Spirit. He spoke of Earth changes and many other things to come. There were many other beautiful angels whom I could see. Some wore large white plumes draped all around their head, while others appeared to wear a golden skull cap.

I felt I had been given a wonderful gift to be able to receive the angels. But in 1983 I received my greatest shock when the Holy Spirit descended. It is an experience you cannot forget and it is like nothing you can ever anticipate. The energy from the Holy

Presence is different from the angels in that it is extremely powerful, yet very loving. I was first aware of a very brilliant light and then tremendous energy entered at the top of my head and traveled all around my body. I felt something important was being delivered through to me and I had to write it down. This was when I received the first message "To Each and Everyone."

From my point of view, the impact of the Divine Presence is a very emotional experience. When the energy of love starts to flow through the body something happens. There is a deep feeling in the energy and it triggers an awakening of some kind. The heavy human veils start to peel away and suddenly, you find you're not the same person. It's as if the Spirit takes precedence over the human part of us. When the second message was given it started to dawn on me that I was being called into service. Later I found out that there are many ways to serve the Divine One, but mainly it's in the willingness to help our fellow beings in any way we can.

By 1995 I realized I had a collection of messages from the Divine Spirit and from Archangel Raphael. I have assembled this book to share these messages with you.

*I sincerely believe there is a much deeper meaning to the messages than can be interpreted through the intellect. Therefore I suggest that this book be read from the heart or through the spirit **slowly**, in order to digest what the Divine One is saying.*

God Speaks His Heart

♥ ♥ ♥

Rev. H. R. McClellan

Where there is Love
there is Peace

Where there is Peace
there is Truth

Where there is Truth
there is Bliss

Where there is Bliss
there is God

TO EACH AND EVERYONE

"Fear not..as you write my words for they bring meaning to my children"

FIRST I MUST tell each and every one of you that I love you very much. When you read my words, you will be filled with the meaning of them. Each one of you has a measure of My love inside. This measure will grow and become very powerful, as My love comes into being within each of you now.

Yes, my beloved ones, I promised you that I would fulfill my prophesy, that being that I would send my son to you again. As I speak these words now, it has already been done, the **way** has being laid open for my son to reach you. He will come to you in a very simple way. . .**each according to their own thinking.**

Beloved ones, yours is the gift I give to you today. By my power, through my words, each one of you that has the mind to receive Me will do so, even as I receive you unto my own heart now.

My children, my vision is complete now, for I have envisioned a peaceful place where we can all live as one together in **love**. The purpose of these words, then, is not to mislead you into thinking my kingdom is that of milk and honey. It is more than that my children, it is **my storehouse of Love.**

Yes, my children, each and every one of you who chooses to listen to my words and accept them for what they are intended to be will receive my gift, that is the gift of themselves.

Each and every one of you is very precious to Me. Each has been given their own worth, and I say unto you now, "look

13

inside yourself and discover that worth". It has been charged to your leaders to take care of you through their own eyes, but I charge you to take care of yourselves. Each and every one of you has the power within to take care of yourself. Would I charge it to a few to take care of the many? No, my children, my power is divided equally among you, because I love each and every one of you.

When you discover the seed of love that is within you, you will discover each other. It is the love that you share with each other, that is the love you share with Me. For the power that I bestow upon you, is the power of **my love**. My love is **NOT** the sword that kills, **but the heart that forgives** with understanding.

Take **not** to the sword my little ones, for each one of my children you kill, so you are killing yourselves. Because each time you choose to destroy, you are destroying **part of Me**, the part of Me that is in yourselves. The Love I have given you will run out of your body, as your blood runs out of your body. Therefore I say, put your love into yourselves and into each other, so it will grow and replenish you, and fulfill you. . .**even as you fulfill Me.**

Put not your love into money, your **love is more precious** than any money. For if your money should run out. . .so shall your love.

Offer not your prayers unto Me, if you cannot offer them unto yourself. For what you ask of Me you will find within your own self. The power of your own heart

be it a GENTLE HEART,
or a COMPASSIONATE HEART,
or a HOPEFUL HEART

14

the power of your **loving heart** will work your miracles. *Even as I watch over you.*

I say a prayer now my children. My prayer is that you come unto Me **empty handed.** For if your hands are empty, then I can fill them. But if they are already full, then I cannot.

Let not my words fear you, **to love is not to fear.** I do not fear any of you, why then should you fear Me?

Courage my children, courage to find yourselves...even as you seek to find Me.

> Let **COURAGE** be your Leader
> Let **STRENGTH** be your Army
> Let **FAITH** be your Flag,

fight for the love that is within you, the love that wants to win the battle, without spilling the blood.

Pour not your blood into the Earth my children, it was not meant for you to do that, for even as you spill another's blood, you are spilling your own blood which is your love. **The love I have given each and every one of you.**

PRAYERS

Let there be Light, so the souls of my children may be
bathed in the recognition of their spiritual roots

I SPEAK TO those who are attuned to My calling now so a greater impetus or stimulation can be given to the masses of humanity who are seeking to understand where they are headed in their life's direction.

My heart is always open to receiving communication from the masses of My children through their dedication to prayers. **Prayers, my children, open the way to deliver recognition between your spirit and My spirit.**

When you pray **in all sincerity**, you are aligning your consciousness with the Divine. The energy of the thoughts, or spoken words, are directed through the veils and are amplified by those prayer angels or messengers who direct the energy toward Me.

Teams of messengers who are in service to Me and My children on Earth then proceed to examine the request to set in motion My power of action. My action in response to the prayers is spiritual. That is, I set in motion what is **beneficial to your spirit on Earth.**

Sometimes My children ask Me to lift them off the Earth because they are not joyous with their life adventures. These

16

children of mine do not understand that they can change the object of their experience through their own creative power. When you are consciously and knowingly linked to My love, and you draw this love energy into your heart and body, the power of My love **is lifting you** even though you may never move from where your feet are placed.

When you draw upon Me from within you, no matter where you live, your outer perspective changes. For then you are not relying upon support from your respective society, but from Me. **You are drawing your guidance from a realm above the power of mankind.**

You must listen and look very carefully at what I give, because **My spiritual way may differ from what you expect according to your Earth way.** When you are in balance and harmony with My Spirit of Love, there is only the feeling of bliss and joy.

Your prayers are **always answered by Me in some measure** and I welcome you to draw upon My Body in your need to be nourished by My guiding light. I serve the need of all of my children when you ask it of Me, for I am always by your side encouraging you to persevere in your Earth life discoveries.

Your life on Earth is not all there is, it is only a passage through a time zone. When you are consciously aware of your inner spirit, you will recognize that you are the traveler passing through a very unique experience. The human experience is challenging to the spirit, but not intended to last forever. It is all a part of understanding the totality of all of life.

SPEAK TO ME OF LOVE

MY BELOVED CHILDREN. The need has come to prepare thyself for I will find a way to show each and every one of My children My deepest love. For some of you, it has been a long hard journey from the place where you started, to where you are now. But I have found it within myself to encourage your splendid endeavors, as you have encouraged Me in your efforts.

It is the time for immense recognition now, for the memory of your spiritual beauty and divineness is already starting to surface. As this memory reaches its fullness, your Earth embodiment will take on that of immeasurable pleasure at the discovery of whom you are in essence.

I speak of your spiritual essence which is like unto a beautiful picture of Me, for I reflect the fullness of your quality. **I have not kept my face hidden from any of you. It is only that you have not recognized it** . But I have been smiling upon each of you since you left my side to seek out other kingdoms, and grow in the understanding of what you discover.

My radiance has always shone forth upon the Earthly Kingdom, so those of you who needed guidance to find your way back, would see the way lighted and the path illuminated. You and I have never been separated in Spirit, for it is my Body of Love which flows through your heart. It is as a reminder that each of you belongs to Me, for I birthed you from my whole spiritual mass, so you could go forth and experience the extent of your desires.

I gave you free will to choose your experiences, because

18

I have ultimate faith in your returning to My Home, My Kingdom. Mine angels gather together to share the joy of seeing you expand and grow mighty in your essence.

It is for you to draw closer to Me now, for I have sent out a **word of recall and recollection**, so those souls who are now ready and prepared to let go, will find themselves being gently guided back and lifted unto Me. And I have waited for this precious moment for eons, my beloved ones so that we may share the immense joy of unconditional togetherness again.

No matter what your chosen path is, I never stop loving you, and I accept you for what you are, my beloved children.

Speak to Me of love, my children . . . speak to Me of love again.

Author's note: I feel God is not asking us to quit our human life and leave the Earth. He appears to be lifting us more toward our conscious spiritual remembrance of Him.

THE SEPARATION

The Tree represents a *symbol* of Me, for I am the Tree of Life, and my children are my fruits on the tree, each fruit encompassing divine nectar, and sweet to the taste. And I gave unto each of my children their own free will to choose. The choice was: to remain on my Tree of Life connected to my nourishment, or to seek out their alternate path to follow.

Some of the children of My Spiritual Body chose to let go of their Tree of Life, and fall to the ground thus creating a duality in the Divine Power.

The Tree of Life, (spiritual sustenance) being removed from the Garden of Eden (idyllic life-consciousness) was *symbolic* of you being plucked from my branches, and from my nourishing sustenance and placed into an unknown environment.

Those who relied upon Me for their nourishment had to find an alternate source of supply. They withdrew unto themselves and looked no more unto Me, but to the Earth for their sustenance. The Earth became their new Father/Mother and they worshiped the Earth as a source of their continuing survival.*

Soon my spiritual offsprings forgot all about Me as their original Father and instead set about proving unto themselves that the Earth's way was all there was.

In their need to be sustained and fulfilled, they were given to plunder, rape, and extract from the Earth every thing it had to offer. They fought over land acquisition, and then over gold. They convinced themselves that the more they took from the Earth

20

and each other, the more powerful they became. In that knowledge they felt secure, and this sense of security gave them something to hold onto, for they had forgotten they were *part of Me.*

Not all of my offsprings survived the separation, many gave up hope and despaired. These soon withered and died, for they had no sense of belonging to the Source of My Divine Love and sustenance. The separation thus created a duality, and My power was divided between those who were *nurtured by Me,* and those who were **nourished by the god-images of their own creative minds.**

So this, my children, is how the great separation took place between us. The remembrance of how you are all part of my Divine Essence has been diminished, as most of my beloved children still look unto the Earth and their respective civilizations for their survival.

Many Angelic Brethren and Teachers were sent unto the Earth to stimulate remembrance, and it was agreed that a Divine Savior would be sent to deliver my children from their forgotteness. Some gave their hearts unto the Christ and were reconnected to their Tree of Life.

It has come upon Me to offer a greater stimulus to my beloved ones. My Seraphim and Cherubim as well as the Archangels, have been readying the pathways into the consciousness of my children. For it is again time for Me to offer myself unto you all, and I will come unto each of you to reclaim what is rightfully mine, mine own children.

Let the prayers of the heart unfold the memories of thine essence so it may be shown how much the love shines between us. Can we begin to understand each other's need, and in that need our life be fulfilled? My life is a flowing estuary of divine nectar for my children to drink, and be nourished with the life-giving forces of joy and bliss. It is my gift that you are by my side as you journey forward, into the discoveries of your tomorrows.

These words are to prepare you to receive Me, when the love may flow again between us, and we will rejoice in the discovery of each other's need. **You are my fulfillment** and I pray, my beloved ones, **that I am yours.**

*In the scriptures Jesus declared himself to be on the Earth but not *of the Earth.*

A MEETING PLACE

TO THOSE OF you who are nearing the preparation time of spiritual awakening, I offer these words to assist: Divine Thought produces Divine Action, Divine Love releases the soul from its bondage. I serve all of you, my beloved children. Look then unto your reflection of Me, so you may become that which you seek through Me.

How can each of you feel My presence around you and working through your life? Beloved ones, wherever you walk, I walk, for there is never a moment when thou has ever been separated from My heart. I reach out, and thou touches Me with thy breath of prayers. I give thee gifts of flowers, as a reminder of thine own beautiful nature.

I see thee standing in the wilderness of thy perplexity, but mine eyes never leave thy face, for nothing is more glorious to behold than the face of the innocent child. I hold thee, my children, in innocence, for thou has searched for Me time and time again, and I have led thee unto the grace of thine own discoveries of thy true nature.

It is but a raindrop from my eyes that washes the deepest mud from thy journeys through time. It was not meant for you to forget Me, even as I cannot ever forget that which is a constant part of Me, My Body of Spirit. You who are so divinely precious in my longing, fill Me with wonder and delight, to gaze upon you and your adventures into the Earth's playground.

Behold, I gave you a flesh temple as a sanctuary for the

spirit, to refresh and regenerate yourself while you continue your journey into the exterior. I encourage you to go into your own inner temple, look into the mirror I have provided, and see yourself as I see you. All the rays of my most brilliant colors become fused together as your essence sparkles with radiant vitality and beauty.

It was my intention that you be as an observer, listening and watching, and joining in the celebration of all of life on Earth. That is why I put windows (eyes) in your temple, so you could peer out and observe the momentum of creation occurring all around you, and so understand your special part in all of My creation.

My children, it is my need now to arrange a meeting place between us. Therefore I have called upon my brightest angels to appear and point the way unto my little ones, toward the place I have chosen for a grand reunion. Hearken to thine inner voice now, for thine essence is a reflection of Me, thy Father/Mother Spirit. For I love thee with the magnitude of all there is, no stronger love abides than what I feel in My heart for My own children.

SANCTUARY

LET US PRAY. We are in communion with each other's energies of love which bind us together as one.

It is a sanctuary which I give thee now, my beloved children, a shelter from the rigors of thy daily existence. It pours forth from My mouth the promise of a place so wonderful that thine heart be fulfilled in all its desires of Me. And unto this sanctuary I will place My light, so you will know it to be a sign unto thine understanding that thy way is lighted before thee.

A tabernacle comes forth from out of the wilderness of thy future, so you may take refuge and find comfort in the knowing that it is I who welcomes you toward the union of our hearts once more. A place so peaceful that it will be as **silence** to thy body, but thy **spirit** will know it as sanctuary.

Thy path has been dusty and laden with many obstacles for you to endure, and you have ventured well and have strengthened thy very soul with endurance. But it is a human endurance which thou hast sought, for thy spirit is gaining its truth by seeking the most for the littlest.

I have sorrowed, that thou hast not called upon Me for assistance. But nay, thou has taken the road strewn with boulders which thou must climb over to continue. This road is never-ending for as soon as one boulder is conquered, another appears. It is better to seek higher ground away from the bombardment of thy earthly woes, and lift thy sight unto its true purpose. It is I you seek at the top of the mountain, and your freedom from the chains that bind you tightly.

I speak of perspectives, of a thinking attitude. It be all prevailing that you set your sights upon an elevated viewpoint, thereby setting in motion a higher more divine road, free from obstacles of your own creation. As you journey forth in life, think not of death, *for I have already seen fit to remove the death ray you so fiercely hold onto.** Therefore I say, be not afraid to consider your life, it is a precious gift I give unto each of my children. Choose to live your life according to the divine principles set down in thine own spirit. For it is better to be joyous than to sorrow, for the life was not meant to be degrading, but uplifting to thy spirit.

Thy flesh body is a reminder of a burden you carry, but it is not a burden which cannot be sampled with joy in the knowing. Let us pray, so our energies of love be united as one and may each find solace in these words I speak. I help thee with thy burden by lightening the load. My unseen hands are stronger and more able to help thee sustain thyself, than for you to carry it alone.

My prayers are answered now, for I have seen a glimmer of remembrance more powerful than before. I unite thee with thy love of Me. My meaning is simple. I am calling in the wilderness of thy forgotten dreams to seek Me out for myself.

Author's interpretation of the death ray: God is making our transition from the flesh easier. When we know that life is eternal, we will not fear our departure from the Earth.

UNITY

Let us pray together now, so the light of our unity flows together as one substance

MY BELOVED ONES. It is given for Me to accept thine offering of prayers and I will now conjoin myself to thine essence, in all truth of the love that shines between us.

When I speak my heart unto my children, it will echo throughout the land, for this is indeed a miracle in itself. It has come for Me to extend Myself unto all who seek Me out, to help you to better understand my nature. I speak words softly so thou will receive them softly into thine own essence.

There has been much harshness accredited to My nature in the past history of humanity. **I have done nothing to rectify this inaccuracy, save send My Son, because it was my wish that humanity's heart be filled with its own compassion for itself.** Therefore I have moved very carefully over the face of my children's destiny so that I not interfere in that which they have chosen to experience among themselves.

There are those who cry out to Me for forgiveness of their nature. I say unto these ones: thou art surely forgiven of Me if thou hast forgiven also thy brothers and sisters and thyself. These words are not new to thee for I have already delivered them unto the Earth plane eons ago.

For those who cannot come unto Me empty handed because they know not what they should give up, I say: Be not afraid of thyself, I will not take anything from thee which is not thine. What I am offering is more than can be realized unto thy humanness. Take heed of thyself, **honor thyself as thou would honor Me, thy humble Father.**

What I give is My love in its purest sense. You have need of Me yes? My love is a gentle breath of new creation. The newness of expectation is all around my children's heads, where it waits until the moment of realization, when it lays to rest in the bosom of humanity.

The moment has come for Me to speak of the relevance of understanding where each one of my children fits into the plan. The plan is very simple: recognition of each other, and of thyself, in **true likeness of Me.**

How long will it take, my children, for you to gather your divineness from where you have scattered it around the Earth? And when you have assembled your divineness, will you recognize **whom you hold within yourself?** My smile is always waiting to encourage you in this endeavor.

Give Me your faith so I may extol thee in closeness--like Father, like child. If you do not know My love, how can you follow in My footsteps? I have already sent My Son unto each of your hearts. I stand ready to raise thee to thy rightful place, by My side.

Oh how I love thee, each and everyone. My peace is forever in your heart when you think of Me.

SUSTENANCE OF LIFE

*The Essence Of The Spirit Of The Divine Shines Forth Its
Light Upon Its Blessed Seed.*

I HERALD THE day must come when I may speak to each and every one of my children. It is my intent to move closer to those who are open to the light of My heart.

It is an ongoing blessing which is given to all those who receive Me now into their hearts. As the Earth changes become more apparent, so will the need to be aligned with the spirit within. For therein contains all the answers to the many questions which will be asked by mankind.

It is a movement of grace which is being set in motion and the many who have become aware of My presence upon the Earth will be aligned to the path of ascension. This is only a procedure which will be very stimulating to the ones who are now preparing to unfold unto their true nature, while still in human embodiment.

The gloriousness of the light of all life will become more apparent as the energy is swiftly moved forward toward the next century. I am suggesting this time as a guideline for reference. To the spirit there is no time, only joy in the living.

As the human race becomes more aware of its spiritual nature, it will start the process of gaining its universal wisdom through those teachers who are preparing to leave my side now, and descend into the flesh, so the gathering of my own can be accomplished.

When My presence is felt more upon the Earth, those who are ready to take their quantum leap will be guided. The rest of humanity is not forsaken by Me. All are blessed in My heart. It is not the moment for their ascension from the planet.

Great changes often occur as the light penetrates the heavy density of mass consciousness. The fighting is not important for survival, it only establishes a progressive thought. It is therefore better to reason before taking up the sword, for it will not accomplish a joyous meaningful life. **Will my children ever learn to feel peace?** Perhaps, when the human emotions and thoughts are silent, then the stillness of the heart will ring out its cry **"love for all of life."**

Accomplishment in human endeavors means nothing to the spirit, who must relinquish the nothing to achieve its all. I cannot tell you not to anger in the emotions, but I can encourage you to love with the heart. **That is where you will find the salvation you are all seeking, within your own heart.**

Love is more powerful than any fighting, for in the love comes the release. If you have to fight, let it be with your heart which is joined unto Mine. For I envision a better way to settle all disagreements without dishonor. It is better to understand the motivation of your brothers and sisters than to punish them by your judgment.

Why do my children argue among themselves? Have I not given each of you enough power to establish your route through life? If you are in need, why have you not called unto Me for sustenance? And in that sustenance is there not life?

I am the Spirit of Life that flows within you, yea even beyond the flesh you value. **And when you lose your flesh, am I not**

30

here to lift you and carry you into a new consciousness-- yea even forgetfulness of your Earth journey? The life never falters it is constant my beloved children, think on this. You leave Me and travel to the Earth, you leave the Earth and travel back to Me. So what is lost? It is all in the understanding of My nature and **your everlasting life.**

VALUES

When my children come unto Me, I shine the light of my love, so your spirit and my spirit fuse together, and we become as one.

When the Spirit of your essence is aligned to the Spirit of my essence, then all will become clear unto you. It is not a matter of time but necessity, of reaching up and accepting that which is rightfully yours, your spiritual inheritance.

It may come as no surprise to many, that a part of Me is inside each of you, it is a light that never dims. Some of you are aware of it, and are consistently expanding this light, so that you become as a spiritual being, as well as a human being. This is all part of the purpose for being born upon the glorious planet, called Earth.

The human experience is sequential in its own right. It merits a closer scrutiny of your actions and feelings, to see if they flow in togetherness. Sometimes the human part of you and the spiritual part go separate ways, and this causes great frustration because neither is achieving the greatness of the life. It is worthwhile to seek the light within you, and look upon its flame, in this way you will be connecting to the light of Me.

I can assist you in furthering your discoveries of your spiritual nature, if you are willing and make an effort. I can only say that the joy at discovering your true spiritual nature is far greater than any of your discoveries on Earth. Nevertheless, every choice you make sets up a reaction on your soul level.

The colors of your Essence sparkle brighter than the glow of distant stars. But you are not a star, you are part of Me. You and I created the Universe together, at that instant **you were still joined to My Whole.** I did not unjoin you from My Body Essence until I felt it was immanent for you to experience multiple sensations while in a flesh encasement.

There are those among you who are already receiving My words directly into their innermost soul. These beloved ones are being guided unto special training so they may become teachers among you, reflecting the glow of your own nature. Glory is something which belongs to everyone and can be attained through the giving to others of my beloved children, in their search for their rightful identity.

Look not to the flesh for your identity, for as with all precious things of mine, they are wrapped and carefully hidden from view until the moment of unveiling. This moment approaches in the history of humanity, for as you seek the spirit so you shall find it. The Earth is only a camouflage, when you have had your fill of the camouflage, you may look **deeper** to see what it hides. In order to be able to claim what is rightfully yours, you must give it your all. That is, you must put **effort** into its attainment, otherwise it will not be **worthy enough** to have any value.

Let us speak together of values. There are My spiritual values, and then there are your Earthly values. Each has its place. You should understand that your Earth values only last you for as long as your journey on the Earth. Whereas the values in your spirit are part of you forever, and are not sacrificed on the battleground of the flesh.

33

These little words are my offering for you today, my beloved children. Think on them well. I love each and everyone of you. You are part of My body. I am your Whole. Blessings to all those who seek Me out.

KINGDOM OF MY HEART

I write in simplicity, so all can understand my words with the innocence of a child

MY BELOVED CHILDREN, as the gleam of recognition of whom you are starts to shine, then the energies of our spiritual nature will pour forth its blessing upon each of you. Be open to receive that which I give you which is My Divine Love.

Each of you has sampled the elements of love in many ways. As a child, a husband or wife, a parent, a brother or sister, this is your human love nature, it is very beautiful. **I wish for you to experience the kind of love which we share, which is of a divine holy nature**. This love I speak of goes beyond any feeling which each of you has experienced before, for its essence lifts you into a very beautiful joining. My essence of love is more powerful than you have received from your human family. It is joy and bliss in the ultimate.

There are those among you on Earth who have strived and put forth great effort ~ some even sacrificing their human nature ~ to connect to this Divine Source of Me. Seeing your determination to receive Me, I have reached down and removed the veil separating human from divine, and have welcomed these children into my arms.

Some others of you are still confused at the difference between human love and divine love. My love, I would say, is a filling up of thy cup until it overflows. It is a measure of ultimate fulfillment, of being at one with the totality of all I have to give. Your human completeness is sharing in the love of the human family. Your spiritual completeness is in the joining of your spiritual self unto mine.

When the human experience is over and you return to the Kingdom of My Divine Spirit, you are reconnected to My Essence, if you so choose.

I speak of your return to your spirit. It is a blessed event that you know Me, and **I come closer to your recognition and understanding of our relationship to each other.**

My heart never stops beating to the rhythm of my children's need of Me. I only ask that you find it within yourself to seek Me out for what I am. In this endeavor you may be surprised for I am not what you consider Me to be. It is my nature to give and to receive all that is forthcoming from time immemorial until no more. When you choose to blend the essence of your spirit with mine, you become **as one with Me. Then you live not alone as an individual, but as part of the largest unity you can ever comprehend.**

I gave each of you your life as an individual unjoined from My mass body of divine love. It was my wish to give you freedom from my side to venture unto those worlds of creation where you would **build upon your inner light** and **create** those things meaningful to your journeys.

Each of you has a need to experience creation, mine and yours. A sampling of this power has taught you to build those masterpieces unto your own expression.

Do you not give your own human offsprings blocks and crayons to assist them in expressing their creativity with their toys of learning? **Thus I gave unto each of you, my beloved**

36

**children, certain of my power to creatively express that which
you sought to bring into manifested learning.**

The building blocks of my power has allowed you to build
yourself, the being you wish to become. For your outer creative
expressions have build the inner you. Do you understand this, my
beloved ones?

Those who serve Me are with a greater creative power. But
my hand guides them in their objectives, so that what they create
is for the betterment of the **Whole of My family,** and not for the
individual self. I have a divine plan of creation ~ you are all part of
that plan since you are part of my body essence, my children. I do
not create for one, but for the Whole. What I say is: one is not
more precious to Me than another.

I have spoken of myself, but now it is the moment to speak
of your relationship to each other's essence. When you look upon
each other you see a reflection of all the races of human. I ask you
now to look **behind** the human face to the spirit within, which is the
Light of My Body. It is a time of reflecting the light you carry to your
spiritual brothers and sisters, so they in turn may know themselves.

Look beyond your flesh, it is only a temporary housing, but
the spirit within you is **forever.**

THE MIGHTY SOUL OF THE CHILDREN

WHEN A MASS effort ensues to link the light of the soul with the light of My Heart, it is then that a dramatic uplifting will occur.

I look upon the mighty soul of the children who are seeking answers to deliver them from the bondage of their flesh. The flesh is an important part of the human existence, for it serves its own purpose. I come to lighten the **heaviness of the none understanding** of life in its unique form. Life is Life. An opportunity to share among each other, all the splendors of My divine love, and in that action a bonding of spirit with spirit is achieved.

When my children feel the deepness of My love and extend it along to their brothers and sisters in an ongoing movement, that is achievement in the highest degree of spiritual understanding. When that knowledge has been absorbed into the mainstream of the human consciousness, then the golden stream shall flow forth.

It is I that speaks My heart unto my children now. Let my gifts be amplified throughout the Earth. A coming together of united energies, mine and thine is a miracle of birth. So say I, from My heart unto yours, let the prayers of communion begin. Set aside all that is not love, so purification can commence. We are in the throes of oneness collectively; a rekindling of the separate spirit to the Whole of Spirit, **in the consciousness of the soul atom.**

Forasmuch as I forgive thee, children of my breath, I ask that you also forgive the actions of your brothers and sisters who are still contemplating their true self. The light of the spirit entwined with the light of the human, equals perfect unity of human existence.

SWORD OF TRUTH

When it is given that each of my children seeks me out for Myself, then I will know that it is time for Me to come from my secret place and make myself known

WHEN WE COME together, our energy combinations provide a Light unto the Earth. It is because I pour through you those things which are needed and necessary on the ever-expanding Earth plane. The Earth has been regraded so it can provide a place of learning for my future generations of children to play and grow in their respective wisdoms.

I seek at this time, to call and collect unto My heart, all those precious ones who will be as my leaders for this very important new generation. These souls will be guided by my energies of love to lead the way toward the unfolding of the understanding of the new laws governing the spiritual evolution of my beloved children.

The way, the truth and the light, will gleam in the hearts and minds of my children, so there will be no doubt about their beauteous spirit within. Mine hand and sword of truth is upon my children now, so that they can be led toward a glorious Golden Era of appreciation of their own worth and value. It is already being accomplished as the Earth's movement projects them into their magnitude of remembrance of Me, their Father of All.

I say now there is no doomsday, and I admonish those who would relish in this misinterpretation of my words. I promised you a New Earth, a New Dawn, a New Day culminating in the Golden Era. Then those of my children who will be present on Earth, will feel fulfilled in their joy by walking alongside each other, in total remembrance.

What I am saying, my beloved children, is that the heavy veils which have been worn over your spiritual eyes will be lifted and the glory of the sight restored. You will each need to refocus your spiritual sight, so you can look through to the beyond of that which has been represented to you as the unknown.

The veils of the human consciousness have served you well and have provided you with a stimulus on your Earth journeys. You will be shown this as you move more into the light of your Golden Era. For you will see through your spiritual sight those things never witnessed through the human senses before.

Each of you will receive my blessing, for you have arrived at the bridge between the human and the spirit. The Spirit of Christ has prepared ye well for this bridge, and he will conduct a special ceremony of light and love to welcome you to this special embarkation of your spirit's journey into the golden ray of sunshine, and your existence on planet Earth will take a dramatic change.

FOLLOW YOUR OWN HEART

THERE IS MUCH discussion among those children of mine who are divided in their thought of whom they should follow. My precious ones, it shall be given unto you to **follow your heart**, for only in the heart is the true expression of the love we both share. It has been My Will to allow you freedom to express your desires in a manner of your choice, therefore allowing you the unlimitedness of thought. It is also My Will to encourage you to seek the light of your soul. For the depths of your essence contains all the memories of your initial conception and birth into individual consciousness.

You and I are the Whole of Life in its entirety. There is nothing I can offer you that is of more value than life itself. Through the experience of the life principle, all of my children are consciously aware of themselves. When you were divided from the Whole of my Spirit, you were born into your own existence. Your conscious awareness was that of an individual aspect of Me, your Creator.

It is by movement of choice that my children progress in the discovery of what all of life has to offer. Myriad opportunities to experience multiple sensations through the human senses, as well as the inertia of the quickening of the soul. As the souls of my beloved ones grow in the experience of everything they desire to create in the learning field, they become enlightened. The lightening is the conscious application toward the growth expansion.

Drawing upon the power of My Body of Light Particles, my children create a variety of forms. The forms represent a soul expressing itself through matter. As the soul learns to master the power of expression wisely, the more it progresses in its expansion. Using the light threads of Spirit to create its movement forward through time, my children direct light through the conscious application. The more light you use, the more stability in the balance between human and soul life. The light is the energy of the soul essence. Projecting the light from the soul into the conscious atoms of the human body form, creates an expansion of intelligent integration. Light-fusion, passing through the molecules of the human form, transcends the density of matter into density of light particles. This constitutes a passing into an enlightened state of mind, body, spirit. The soul is increasing the vibratory rate of escalated light particles.

Are you aware your soul has a vibratory rate? It is the ratio of the speed of light passing through your human body. Are you knowing of the speed of light? Each spirit body is comprised of electromagnetic light waves. Re-energized means a fusion of light introduced into the cortex of the brain. Your human brain needs light to function in its fullest capacity. My beloved ones, Christ demonstrated his magnitude of light. When you return again to my realms, you will be totally immersed in light.

Come unto Me beloved generations of My Body Spirit, so I may give thee my blessedness. Begin to understand that I come to deliver my children from that which binds them to the Earth's calling. Let thine own spirit emerge into the light of understanding its place in Me, so I may prepare to receive my beloved ones, into the brilliance of a new spectrum of discovery.

That which has been said before will be given for reflection, as mine eyes hold the vision of completeness. Come forth from within thy shell and reflect thy brilliance, so the Earth can be filled with its illumination. I come to bid you extend your heart until it is filled with My Heart undivided. Then we walk together, not in the shadow of life, but in the reflection of divine joy at being united as one. I am in thy spirit. Thy spirit is in Me.

ALL SPIRIT OF MY BODY IS DIVINE

WHEN YOUR SOUL is struggling to understand its own self-worth, it willingly sets up a mirrored image (alter ego) to compare itself to. This alter ego image, is only an illusory reflection of itself, and must not be confused with its true image, which is beauty.

After comparing itself to its illusory reflection, your soul may attempt to reclassify its worthiness. If the soul establishes an **inner knowingness**, it will overcome its ego reflection, thereby bypassing its human flesh body. All this is a continuation of your soul's inherent need to discover its relationship to Me, its Divine Source.

If I were to tell you that you are each Divine, would you believe Me to the fullest degree? And in that belief, would you live the remainder of your life as a divine being in a human form? Believing in yourself is a prerequisite to a joyous life, and will aid the soul to gain its fundamentals of truth within itself. Therefore I say, do not accept or reject these words but **know** who you are, by **discovering your own essence**, which is My Essence, delivered unto the Earth plane.

I am thee, thee are Me. What more is there for Me to say unto you, except *forget me not*. I am not about to disappear from your life, **for I am the life in you**, my precious children. You see, I love that which is Myself, My own body of Spiritual Essence. You are walking on Earth as my representatives. Each of you is representing My Divine Nature. Your human training may inhibit your thinking, **but that part of Me, which is your Spirit, knows its true birthright.**

I have been calling you on the path toward home for some considerable time. You have become so used to the Earth you consider it your only home, but this is not truth, as it is only a temporary structure.

Be not afraid of your spiritual home. You were not afraid to leave Me to go yonder to explore, and in that exploration came growth of understanding of a physical existence. But you are still spiritual, you have only forgotten your nature, because you have explored so far, and have lost your bearings. Traveling on and on, you have ceased remembering the place where you started, and so you have gone around in circles.

But I knew that when time was immanent, having traveled in a circle, you would eventually return to the place where you started. And here I am, to welcome you back, as if you have never been far. You have carried a life thread with you which is attached to Me, so you could really never get lost.

Some have ventured into the deepest caverns just to see what was there, and were unable to find their way out. Nevertheless, **the life thread is strong**, and you have only to pull on the thread and I will lift you out of the cavern and back into the safety of My home.

Although I extend a hand to those in need, I will not pull you. You must want to be lifted. I would not retract you without you asking it of Me.

This is only to let it be known that I wait patiently at the place where you started, where you are always in My sight.

DIVINE HEALING

MY BELOVED CHILDREN, I have nothing to give you that is more precious than My Love, which I ask that you accept into your heart. In this way you will be full of Me.

My love is the most powerful medicine the Earth needs to heal itself. As the Earth heals so will my beloved children also heal in their soul's understanding of who they are in relation to Me. This healing through my love, will enable all to come unto My spirit in a more purified way.

What is occurring, is a bypass of the route which many of my beloved children are presently taking. You see, many are taking the long circle home, but there is a much shorter route, through the healing elements of the soul. As each soul is healed of its Earth life conditioning, it is lifted up unto a new authority. This authority is gentle, and will not subject them to any more harsh treatment than they have experienced in their life's domain.

It has been recognized by Me that my beloved children need assistance to open up more fully their spiritual reality. As my children become more attuned to their own soul and recognize its very beautiful nature, they will aspire to recognize their roots in Me. The more my children are aware of their own spirit, the more they will recognize themselves in Me, since I am part of their spirit. Therefore, I am encouraging the *healing of the human spirit* to take place.

A combined healing is already in progress through the efforts of my precious Angels and their dedication to the uplifting of the human race, and the Earth system. All of my beloved children are provided for, they need only to look deeply, and discover the powerful love flowing freely through the heart. All of this action is gently guiding my children back into their remembrance of Me. I provide the Light of the Ages, so those souls who are ready, will be instantaneously bathed in this light.

So you see, my beloved ones, I am the means to the ultimate discovery that all of you are progressing toward. **For each soul must return from whenst it came,** it is all part of my divine way. That all souls be free to explore whatever galaxy they choose, and from that exploring, they grow bigger and bigger in their total understanding of everything in existence.

If all my children lived only on the Earth plane, then their discoveries would be very limited to the human experience only. Therefore not wishing to limit my children's growth, I gave them a choice of many galactic regions, and star systems*, where they could be born and live very diversified lives.

I also gave them the power to create upon their planetary system the type of life adventure which pleased their individual spirit. And my children have grown out of these adventures and have matured in their spiritual nature. Many have taken on a greater responsibility, that of becoming a big brother or sister to the rest of My family.

It has become my wish to reach my children and I have sent my emissaries unto the Earth to prepare the way. FOR WHEN I SPEAK MY MESSAGE TO EVERY ONE OF MY CHILDREN, ALL WILL HEAR ME. For My light will project into each and everyone's soul, and become a turning point in their spiritual growth.

All of my beloved children are very precious to Me because you share my body of spirit. My message of love will reverberate through all of the human veils, until it reaches the core essence of the spirit. Have you not considered how precious you are to Me, my children? For without you, my children, I could not be.

Fear not what you have heard of the Earth changes. Creation means change, and the Earth plane is being molded and prepared for its journey into the next millennium. So I say unto you now, beloved ones, enjoy that which you have, but be always ready to let go, for nothing on Earth is forever. The Earth must continue to replenish itself; you must also replenish yourself and move forever onwards in the direction of your discoveries.

* Author's note: Although other life forms have yet to be discovered on other planets in the Universe, it does not exempt our findings in the future.

MY LOVE IS SHARED BY ALL

I SPEAK MY message to my beloved children who are searching for Me in their deepest understanding of their present Earth life, and in their soul's gains through and by their endeavors for Me. I plan to reach as many of my children in the forthcoming time, so that they may be cherished by Me and feel my deep love entwined in the essence of their being.

It is a time of uniting, of bonding together as one Light. These words are intended for those who cry out to Me in the suffering of their physical bodies, and their none understanding of the Earth's way, in the form of teaching of the soul. Let the life lessons begin to reflect the understanding in the human consciousness, so the Spirit of my children can be uplifted forever.

I speak My Heart also to the very little ones who have suffered much pain and torment, and have gained nothing from the none compassion of the unlearned. **Let the suffering of my very little ones be recognized by those beloved souls who are ready and willing to set free unto their own life's evolution:**

- The mammals, reptiles and flying animals, and all that comprise these families.
- The marine life, and all that comprise this family.
- The insects, and all that comprise this family.
- The plants, trees and flowers, and all that comprise this family.

♦ The remaining animals of each distinction,
  and all that comprise these families.
♦ All other nonhuman life forms and their
  families, who have not been included in above
  Love.

Let those who give assistance to these life forms on behalf of Me, be blessed by My Spirit, and feel My presence in and around them giving comfort.

Let My words be blessed as the one writes them in faith of Me. The light shines forth on the Earth and all who see and feel it, will also see Me.

Given in Love to all my beloved children, through the Grace of My Heart.

INNER FULFILLMENT

THE ENERGY of love is upon you, my beloved children, it is this energy movement that I ask you to consider now.

When the whole of humanity becomes as one with love, then it is that ingredient which becomes predominant in the mainstream of life's achievement. For what is life if it cannot be filled with love from within the understanding of the purpose it serves? I love all of my beloved children, that is a truth which is undeniable. I love all that is mine to give. Total fulfillment of the precious journey of life, leading the inspiring spirit toward its discoveries of its needed experiences and continuing ever forward through its passage of time.

These words I speak to each of you now, are but a fragrance. Fragile in its structure, it delicately perpetuates its nature by acceptance of its touch. As long as it is accepted for its beauty, it lingers around the recipient for all to breathe in its purity of essence.

You see, my beloved children, I give thee many gifts. Some are invisible to the human eye, only the inner spirit can detect the miracles of knowing they exist. It is all that I have to offer to a wondering soul. Notice I did not say lost ~ it is only the human judgment which is lost in the folds of its sentient values. The soul of each of my children, wherever it chooses to wonder, is only seeking to push itself to its limits. A test of its nature? Perhaps it only seeks to understand the power it possesses.

It is to be understood that the power of My body is **forgiveness** in the ultimate. I forgive each of you for not recognizing your own spiritual love for yourself and each other. **You have allowed the seeds of your human perspectives to grow out of proportion to the seeds of your spiritual roots.** Love is life's purpose, to nurture that which it cherishes the most ~ the foundation from which it derives its nourishment.

My spirit is, and will always be. As part of Me, your spirit is, and will always be. The recognition of your spirit in Me will ease your discomfort. **Until you progress beyond your beliefs in human and refocus your beliefs in your spirit, the games of winners and losers, and survival of the fittest can only remain in the consciousness of human none understanding.** Do you think with the head of your flesh body, or the heart of your spiritual essence? The flesh, which was bestowed upon you freely by your human family, cushions you in your dense environment, and assists you in your discoveries.

But here am I, watching and waiting for your remembrance of the joy of knowing we are part of each other. **That which I created in love can never be separated from Me.** But were I to reveal all that is truth in spirit, what would you gain? For you have to learn *what spiritual truth is*, and unless you attune yourself to recognizing that part of you which is Me, then you will not *understand who created you and for what purpose*.

It is very different from what you can realize through your present human comprehension. Understand that a **realization far greater than where you presently cultivate your expectations, rests in your Essence.** Without the knowledge of spirit, the human life serves no avail, since it reaches a **dead-end.**

All of My creation has meaning and purpose. **Would I give of Myself to that which is nothing?**

I have called to you on the mountain top, in the deserts, and the valleys. My voice has echoed through the depths of the oceans, and in the stillness of each passing cloud. Can't you hear me calling *I love you?*

DIVINE RIGHT

What is between Father and Child is a link
which can never be broken.

I DO NOT send any of my children into war, neither do I fight. It is my nature only to **LOVE**, and allow my children their freedom of expression in their own way. Whatever you are proving, it is unto your own soul. None have to prove themselves to Me, for I know each and everyone. Did I not birth you of My own body?

I recognize all of you my children. It is for each and every one of my children to recognize Me.

55

HOLY PRESENCE

LET US PRAY. Divine goodness pours through to the Earth now as My will is set in motion, benefiting all my beloved children.

Now that my children are more open to receiving Me into their hearts and lives, it will become apparent that I am moving them unto the place of their divine loving nature. This will be sensed more as the Holy Presence comes closer to **each one** and is felt gently moving among my people. The Spiritual Presence is linking up to the spirit of the human family.

I have so much to give unto thee, my beloved ones. Will you accept this offering now so I may lift thee into a golden Light reflecting my peace and grace?

Recognizing thine own essence is only the first step unto deliverance from the chains that bind thee unto thine own human thinking. Raise up now, I say, take up thy position in consciousness, so I may recognize thy readiness to move forward unafraid toward the golden dawn of knowing thy roots in Me.

Simple knowing is a gift unto itself, for when the moment comes to lift thee, all will be ready for the journey into the glorious future I have prepared. Reside in peace and tranquility, so you may experience the Love of the Divine Presence among you.

THROUGH THE EYES
OF LOVE

BELOVED CHILDREN. Mine eyes are thine eyes, for what you behold surely is . . . even unto My own heart. You shall come, and I shall receive each of you in much splendor, for I have prepared a special place in My heart. And you shall know Me, even as I know each and every one of you, my children.

Dearest ones, how can I tell you that you be more than loved . . . you *are* love, **for I have placed within each of you the seed of my heart,** which is my deepest love.

Wherever you shall walk, whether in the fields or on my tallest mountain, the seed of my love is always within you. It is as a light which each of you carries with you to show the way to the others who will look to you to follow.

I am the flow of Life within you. The flow never ceases for there is no end to life, it only changes its course. Would you wish to spend your entire existence on Earth never knowing the joy and ecstasy of other places and other feelings of life within many forms? * To those who have never alofted in the air and soared through space cannot image the experience of the feeling. You see, my children, I want you to experience everything. So you can grow in that experience, and as you grow you become more fulfilled in your being as I am fullilled in mine.

It is said that behind every cloud there's a silver lining, but I show you even behind the silver lining to where lies the ecstasy of knowing the beyond of the little planet you live on now.

If you were to take mine hand, and I were to take you to places beyond your comprehension, would you be afraid? Would you be afraid even if my own hand were tightly in yours and you could not fall or be hurt in any way? Would you be willing to take the opportunity to experience all the beauty thine eyes can behold, and all the joy that lies ready to be unfolded within thee?

The Earth body you carry binds you to the Earth. But My body, the Spirit, allows you freedom to be.

* note: In another chapter, God speaks of creating
     forms other than human.

NEW GARDEN OF DELIGHTS

IT IS A garden of delights which I give thee my beloved ones. When you are ready to walk in my garden, I will make ready the path for each of you to take. All paths lead unto my garden and each of you has a place there in which to grow your own individual very beautiful flowers.

The colors and varieties of the flowers are your own chosen design, and you will receive the seeds to plant these flowers. It is for you then to stand back and watch the flowers grow into their own individual beauty. I will be the one providing all the nourishment the flowers need. It will be a spectacular sight with each and every specie of flower in existence growing in the soil of my garden and I will bless each and everyone for the planting thereof.

This is what I envision now, the Earth blooming in its glory of beauty reflected by the seeds of the children. This can only be accomplished by my children in a combined effort, working together for the same effect, that of planting and growing.

This shall be my new garden of Eden, when my children are ready to restore the beauty of the **initial thought** to its rightful place.

PEACE

PEACE, PEACE, MY beloved children, that is what I ask of you now. My heart is empty without my children's love for Me. I speak these words so that they will reach into the depths of thy being, for that is where I am.

I rest inside of thee, in the depths of thy soul, thy essence. For this is My home, My place of bounteous love which you and I share as one.

As long as I am in thy heart, my rightful place, I will always walk with thee and comfort thee in thy hour of need. But you must be aware of where I am, so you can find your place in Me.

Thou dwells in Me and I in thee, my beloved children. Look not outward but **inward** for Me, and I shall wait patiently until you are ready to come home, so that we may share the greatest love story of our life.

My home, which is thy home, is furnished with all the abundance of thy needs. I wish to share this abundance of love with you. My home is empty without you. Your home is also empty without Me. We each need the other, because we are a part of each other.

That is why I say . . . *peace, peace* my beloved children, so you may hear My heartthrob beating out its message to come and receive Me in our home in the heart. It is there you will see Me forever, as I am.

Christ's Message

CHRIST WILL COME AS A SERVANT TO ALL

"And whomsoever shall follow me, Him shall I lead unto his unfolding"

WHEN IT IS a moment of joy to behold, then I come as a servant unto humanity. For it speaks for itself, that the love we all share as one family, be amplified a thousandfold until there is no doubt upon mankind God is indeed love on the threshold of unity with his beloved children.

It is only when the deepest love of the inner spirit is allowed to find its sanctuary in the heart of the human, then all of the understanding necessary to unite the total being who walks upon the face of the Earth, will be complete.

I have waited for this very precious moment since I withdrew from the Earth to take up my position in the spiritual kingdom. It is a blessing which I give unto all those who are looking unto Me to lead them toward the guiding light of the Father. There is nothing more precious than being **one with God.**

I will be in constant communion with those who draw upon my energies at this important time of preparing the way for the **Holy Spirit to reach the human family.**

CHRIST'S MESSAGE OF FREEDOM

THE LIGHT OF our sharing is unlimited in its perpetuation. When the moment of recognition comes unto my people, then I shall return to their hearts once more.

I speak of claiming what is rightfully yours, beloved ones. I am rightfully yours. **My Father is rightfully yours**. To hold us tightly within your heart is a sign of your acceptance into the Kingdom. For you have agreed to link your body to mine in full motion of the Life Force which flows throughout the Earth and back from whence it came.

It is intended for you to express freedom in that manner which you so choose. It is **freedom** upon which liberty is born. Freedom to live the life you chose, and to experience your creative joy at your own merit.

Arise then, from your ashes once more to peel away the scars of survival. Smell the sweetness of your breath and examine your hands, for they hold your life's worth.

Be not assailed by what pours forth from your neighbor's throat. It is only a warble to Me, for I watch and know what is in each of my beloved one's mind and heart. I see all your tomorrows before you have even awakened from your sleep. I know where you tread, and what you seek, it is as evident as if it were written upon any tablet. Your essence reveals your nature for all of the spiritual kingdom to behold. None can hide their thoughts, desires, motives, for it is projected forth in their ether. Nothing is hidden from my eyes. Do you think your Father does not know where all of his children are in their thinking?

It is a morsel of knowledge I give you to chew upon, as sweet as the nature of My love.

Archangel Raphael

Angels

The angels have already begun to pave their way into our hearts by touching the consciousness of mankind's thinking, gently guiding us into the dimension of the spiritual unknown.

Here, glorious Beings clothed in light, are living a wonderful life, and perhaps having a grander experience than our own.

The joy and love from the Celestial Angels is already lifting our spirit through beautiful doorways of inner light, into a greater understanding of our total whole being.

* * * * * * * * * * * * * * * *

The first time I saw Raphael, I couldn't believe anyone could be that gorgeous! He had been teaching and helping me grow in my spiritual unfoldment since 1980. I had heard his very kind and gentle voice speaking to me through the mind, often encouraging me through many difficult situations . . . but I had never seen his face.

Then one day in 1994, I saw a glowing light and in the center of the very brilliant light was the image of a face. I found myself staring into two large green-blue eyes which sparkled like faceted gems. His lips were slightly parted as if he was about to say something. I could see that Raphael's nose was small and straight and underneath his eyes, almost resting on the cheekbone, there were some kind of gold markings. His silky blonde hair cascaded down to his shoulders in a loose wave.

With the light flowing through this image, there was no doubt in my mind it was a celestial angel with the most beautiful face I had ever seen. (Later on Raphael emphasized that he is a being of pure light. Since he serves both the human male and female gender, he **blends part of both** into his image.) Raphael plays down his beauty. In his own words he puts it this way: "What you see is the beauty of the **Creator** flowing through me. It is God who is very beautiful, because this is his nature."

Nevertheless, I was so impressed by what I saw, I was determined to capture his image on canvas. I spent more than six months looking for the right artist, many couldn't or wouldn't touch the project. Then, just as I was about to give up, I "discovered" a write-up in a magazine about a visionary artist who painted angels. As soon as I spoke with this man on the telephone, I knew he was the right one to paint Raphael. He agreed, and three months later, I had a portrait which bears an exceptional likeness to the Archangel. The portrait is called "The Light of His Countenance."

What I have discovered about Angels.

They are very kind, gentle and humble. They give of themselves in love, if we are in need of their help, especially if we call upon them. Their goodness is part of their service from God to humanity. However, their help should never be abused or taken for granted.

Raphael can travel faster than the blink of a human eye, but he does not have wings. Some say 'wings' were invented by artists around 300 A.D. perhaps to differentiate between human and angel, also to indicate that they can travel very fast. Brilliant colored rays of energy surround the Archangels and these rays could be mistaken for wings. Raphael explains how they travel so fast in the next section of this book.

The angels want us to know more about their life, their world, and form, so we can more readily understand their nature. That is why they have volunteered information about themselves in the pages that follow.

THE LIGHT OF OUR FATHER

It is a wondrous achievement that is occurring in your present era, for we are again extending our hands, and this time you are allowing our love into your lives existence. Each moment you are open to receiving us into your hearts, we are lifting you higher into the light of understanding that we exist. The ones who are already ascending are aware of our realms, our home, and we welcome all.

There was a time when the Earth blocked out all of our light because those on Earth were unknowing of angels and were not of the thought to follow our examples. We do not seek to disturb the journey of the soul upon the Earth, but we are always watching and interfacing with our beloved brethren when it is asked of us. Sometimes our assistance serves only in a temporary way, if the ones who call upon us do not maintain the light we give within themselves. If they return to their same attitude and thought patterns, then they will again draw the negative flows from their surroundings.

We are encouraging humanity to understand more about light and energy in order to comprehend the Kingdom of God. God's Spiritual Body is an intense magnitude of pure radiant light. The rays from God's Body of Infinite Light are so brilliant and powerful, the **intensity** has to be filtered down through those heavenly hosts who are able to gravitate the light so all can receive the flowing of the grace.

The light which is projecting from God is pure. Angels are givers of light. We project light upon the path of the soul. We also aid in the healing, but we are primarily distributors of God's light upon the Earth. The light of our body is contained in its mass, this means each and every one of us in our natural form of spirit is a mass unto itself. As we grow in wisdom, our body becomes more **brilliant.**

We live in unlimited space connected to a large unit of light measurement. In this way we can project and amplify the light waves into the body of the ones who call upon us for help.

When we are communicating our knowledge to you on Earth, a golden sphere of energy passes between us transforming all that it touches into a brilliant spectrum of colors and design. It is this energy feeling passing through the human body which allows for inspiration.

All thought is energy being projected forth from the God plane throughout the universe. God is continually beaming out signals unto his children, whether his spirit children are in a human body form or other kind of form.

If you are open to receiving, the human brain waves can pick up the Creator's signals and receive God's messages, or other sources of inspiration. The human brain can also block the Creator's signals, or shut down, thereby only receiving input from the Earth's surroundings.

The human brain is constructed to absorb light, allowing it to pass through the brain waves into the rest of the body form. From our vantage point we can see this energy spectrum moving in and out of your body. You may not be able to see its patterns with your human eye, but your spiritual eyes can behold this wondrous radiance.

When we give our light transfusion into your brain waves, cellular structure and auric field, we are linking you up to a greater

69

source of light ~ our Creator. We are recharging your spirit through your conscious life lines. Your thoughts are magnetic waves of energy passing through your environment. If your thoughts are loving and happy, then you are passing this degree of energy along to all the people you come in contact with. When you gather together in groups, try to generate light thoughts, then your Earth will radiate its brilliance.

There are more of us than there are of you on Earth. Planet Earth is small, and only a given number of souls live there if a flesh body is provided for them. Would it surprise you to know that the size of the Earth is like one grain of sand in comparison to the enormity of the Kingdom of Spirit? Are you aware that the Spiritual Kingdom is a dimension of never-ending space of unlimited supply?

The point of entry into the Kingdom of God from the human plane is the most crowded because many people departing the Earth still have their attention focused on where they came from. Some have relatives or friends whom they wish to stay close to, or they still feel an attachment to the Earth, for whatever it has to offer. These beings of spirit, until they can let go of the human thought, stay close to the point of entry.

I have primarily spoken of angels because that is what I am. But the masters, saints, brotherhoods, and hierarchies all work together as a team. We follow the guidelines of the plan set forth by the Creator. We all serve in our capacity as amplifiers of the spiritual values.

70

THE LIGHT OF OUR WORLD

I AM A reflection of the Holy Father's grace and it is my intention to bring this divine beauty of the Father and His Glory unto the children of the Holy Essence. We will be interfacing with the many in an uplifting way, so the divine children of God may begin to see the beauty of God reflecting through their essence also.

Where there is God there is always an abundance of beauty because this is the Holy Father's nature. This is one of the many gifts which our Father gives to us. We know we are a part of God's divine energy and radiance and we swell in this knowing.

What we are intending to do is bring God's energies closer to humanity and entwine them with the children on Earth so they may experience the divineness of the feeling of joy as the Father conjoins with his children. It is a moment of wondrousness to behold as we see, from our realms, God's radiance reflecting through his children on Earth.   This is only a small part of the ascension, and I would say that once the soul is stimulated to step upon the ascension path, it will be like an elevator gently lifting the souls toward their highest point of light which they can com- fortably tolerate.

Let me speak of that now. Light which you can comfort- ably tolerate. The light projecting from the Father's Body of Pure Spirit is so powerful, so pure, so radiant, a more dense body cannot tolerate the brilliance.   The light passes through and breaks down all that is not pure.

Think of yourself living in a dark cave all of your life, your body having adapted to this dark environment. If you should one day, step outside of your dark cave into the brilliance of the sunshine, think of the effect upon your eyes, your senses. Your body will immediately react to the brilliance of the light. You may only be able to tolerate the sunshine in small doses until your body has adjusted to the new environment and you can comfortably accept the rays of the sun.

It is the same when you are lifted in ascension. We, the angels, serving the Father, can only introduce you to minute amounts of light until your body has adjusted and stabilized to the new wave lengths. We allow you to rest while your dense flesh is adjusting to its new radiance. You may feel a temporary discomfort, tiredness, or other imbalance until your cells and membranes adjust to the new vibrational level. You are vibrating to the speed of light passing through your body. **We are ever-increasing the speed,** and so you may feel disorientated or experience lapses of memory.

Your memory is like film in a camera upon which is stored the pictures of everything that has come to your awareness. If your memory-film is suddenly exposed to brilliant light, it can erase some of the images. This is what happens when your brain waves absorb an above normal infusion of light particles.

The angel's body of light waves vibrates at a speed much faster than your flesh body. That is why you cannot see us through the lens of your human eyes, because they are not designed to capture the light speed at which we travel.

72

Your human eyes are suitable for your planetary environment and your dense body form. Therefore, if you desire to see us, you will need to focus your spiritual eyes. Because our eyes are used to brilliant light infractions, we also must wear a lens covering our sight if we wish to observe you in your flesh* form.

In order to understand your inner spirit, you must understand light and energy rays. Those of you who are already seeing with your spiritual eyes will be able to detect the inner spirit leaving at the time of death of the flesh body form.

Your outer flesh form is very suitable for your Earth journey. However when it is time to leave you must discard your flesh because the spiritual kingdom is a very high-vibrational light dimension, and your flesh would immediately disintegrate.

Upon entering our spiritual realms, although you have no flesh body, you may still see yourself and your relatives in the human form. This is because your **flesh form is still predominant in your immediate thinking** and so your spirit projects or creates this image like a hologram.

You are no longer human, you are spirit. Your spirit body is an **essence.** There is no breath, no heart beat, no stomach to fill, no organs to create children. You will immediately feel the loss of weight of the heavy flesh. Then there is a period of readjustment to a very **different** life existence. You will find you can travel very quickly from one place to another. Once you are acclimatized, you will find there is much to do, and even more to learn.

~~~~~~~~~~~~~~~~~~

*Author's note: The Archangel has explained that without the lens, the angels can only see the energy rays comprising our subtle body. Our flesh is too dense for them to see through *their* eyes.

OUR PURPOSE

I AM Archangel Raphael, leader of a great number of angels. These brethren are my divine helpers who work continuously for the betterment of the soul.

We are in constant alignment with the Creator, since we all serve God to the highest degree of our empowerment. Specially appointed, as overseers of the development of Earth and the human race therein, we serve with love and joy.

My angels are divided into groups, each serving a specific function, such as healing or aligning the soul with its pathway. Some are assigned the very difficult task of communicating with those on Earth who are linked unto our message center. This is a place that monitors spiritual dimensions of space and whole races of life forms to determine movement and formations. We look ahead to envision future destinies of life forms to see where their thought patterns are leading them.

We monitor all souls collectively to ensure that the mass intent is progressing toward the Divine Plan. Each Being lives its life as an individual, unaware that it is part of the whole unit of spirit on Earth. When we look upon the Earth, we see spirit as light in motion. Part of our responsibility is to keep the light constant so that it does not go out.

Many humans, unaware of the laws of creation, consider their present home to be indestructible, and without considerable

74

thought, they often take it for granted. But it is a system that is very delicately balanced by life giving energies. When you are born upon the Earth, you carry within you a very important responsibility, which is respect for your own life and for the life of the star system you occupy.

The time of mass movement toward unity is ever present, and will assist the future generations of souls planning to enter the Earth life system to complete their missions in a more direct and positive way. Whenever there is unity in mass form it takes less directed energy to move toward a specific goal, because there is no opposing force to detract from accomplishment.

EARTH CHANGES

MY PRECIOUS BRETHREN the changes you are progressing through are all part of the re-creation of the Earth. The planet you live on is very important to the growth of the many species of life. The Earth is slowly being healed and reborn into a new dimension of light. The light will be like nothing which has ever been experienced on the Earth before.

Through an infusion of light particles we are gradually raising the Earth to Heaven. This does not mean the Earth will leave its orbit. What it does mean is that it is being progressed into another dimension. The darkness, or negative energy which has surrounded the planet for eons, is being transmuted into a lighter sphere.

We call this phase *ascending,* because the Earth is gradually being accelerated into a faster vibration. This means the ratio of the speed of light passing through the Earth is increasing in momentum. Gradually, as the light expands, it will envelope everything in existence on the planet.

Remember conquering the sound barrier? You are about to conquer the light barrier. When you do, you will be able to travel through the dimensions. But this is still further ahead in your future.

All who have chosen to be born, or stay on the Earth at this time, will go through a transition. The human body, as well as other specie of life, is already adapting to the changes taking place. Some are already accelerating into a less dense body. This may not necessarily become obvious to the naked eye. Nevertheless you will **feel** differently.

If you have chosen to be a part of the transition into light, it means you, your body and your lifestyle such as it is, will be undergoing expansion. What this means is dramatic changes will occur. Perhaps you have already let go of the old. Many of you are already becoming consciously aware that your life is not the same as it was perhaps five or ten years ago. Some have experienced the sensation of everything being speeded up. This is occurring not only to humans but to all species of life.

We the angels, who are surrounding the planet, are of the thought that there will be no doomsday, only a new Earth more wondrous than before. You are in your final journey through the transition from dark into light.

Those of you who have awakened to the call of my trumpet will be more consciously aware of the movement from the old into the new. It is not a time of fear but of joy. You have already come far from where you entered the Earth's sequence and your birth onto the beautiful planet Earth. It is beautiful, is it not? Take a moment to recognize all the beauty which you are part of.

The Earth was created as a wondrous unique place for you to explore in your journeys through time and space. And it has provided a haven for you to create and grow from the many human experiences encountered.

The Earth itself is made up of trillions of life forms all living their own existence according to their individual expression. All species of life have the opportunity to re-create their likeness and propagate their own form. The Earth itself is a living, breathing, planet with all species of life carefully interlocked to provide for the growth and continuation of the planet itself.

Our Father is very joyous of all of the species representing Him on Earth however small or unevolved. I would say now that each life form has to start somewhere in its growth, otherwise there is no learning. All species learn by experience. As the human race develops intellectually, it is becoming more aware of its own flesh body with the recognition of its own part in total creation.

The planet is now being cleansed and reborn into a new Earth. Some of the species you are used to seeing may disappear and new life forms take their place. As the Earth becomes more infused with light particles and becomes less dense, the forms which cannot adapt will leave. This will make room for other 'light' forms to appear and develop into new types of species.

The human form is also adapting through this transition. Beloved brethren the Earth is constantly changing all the time. Mountains have risen while other land masses have become swallowed up by the oceans. This has been occurring ever since it was created by the Father. The Earth **must replenish itself** through the changes or it would stagnate and die.

Fear not, God is not planning to destroy the Earth but **SAVE IT**. That is why it is being healed and cleansed and reborn.

PREPARATION

The moment is approaching when all on Earth will become aware of the presence of the most Divine One. Preparations are now becoming focused to lay the groundwork for the movement of energies to lighten to the calling of the most high. Listen and prepare for the moment is at hand.

It has been a mighty changeover from the mass of darkness unto the spectrum of light which is now starting to prevail around the planet. We look upon the Earth as being reborn into a new star. Many of the old decaying ideas and thought forms which lay heavy upon the consciousness of the planet, are slowly being transmuted into energy molecules of a lighter density.

Spatial interconnecting with the gravitational pull has allowed the lifting of the heavy density into a lighter geometrical formation. There is also a linking up of system structure within the spectrum of the closest galaxy. (This will soon be demonstrated through the eyes of those scientifically attuned to the planetary movement.) What I am speaking of is drawing the Earth into a universal formation in preparation for future generations of travelers.

We are in the throes of oneness collectively. This means a rekindling of the separate spirit to the Whole Spirit, in the consciousness of the soul atom. The light of the spirit entwined with the light of the human, equals perfect unity of human existence.

I encourage you now to set aside all that is not love, so purification can commence.

HOW WE SEE HUMANITY

WE ARE THE the hosts speaking in the light of the Golden Kingdom of God.   We are in attendance to the Earth's cry of our beloved ones. We hear the voices, the murmuring of the masses, it is passed through to us beyond the veils separating human from its own spirit. We come forth from our dimension to assist in the understanding of the movement of the forces light and dark upon the beautiful planet.

What we see is different from what you see. We behold the **radiance of the energy** comprising the human and ethereal form. We look closely at this energy for it **foretells where the thinking of the individual is leading the soul.** From our visual point which is far above the planet, we can focally penetrate the darkness to the very core of the Earth. We can also foresee where the thinking of the whole world is proceeding, by the way the energy is lifting or falling. It is like a searchlight focused ahead of the movement of the masses. Thoughts are energy, they can light up or darken the whole planet. Be aware of your thoughts, for the lighter your thoughts the more positive the subsequent behavior. The light lifts the eyes of the soul beyond its present boundaries.

The light of Christ is always focused upon humanity's intent, so the goodness in the hearts of the many can prevail. **Do you understand how important the light is to reflect onto your own future destiny?** When your thinking action is in the light of

God, it is that motion which sustains and carries you forward. The ones who prevail in the darkness through their own choice, become lost in the tunnel.

If you will allow it, we will assist you by shining a glorious light through the end of the tunnel to show you the way out. No soul seeks to be lost, for it means you do not know where you are headed. Therefore, you walk blindly through your God-given life of joyous opportunity, not understanding where your footsteps are taking you. Relying upon chance or luck places you on uncertain ground. And that ground you put your trust into can often break up and disappear. It is important for the soul to **instinctively** know it is connected to the guiding light of the Father.

It is a time on Earth of teaching the many the simplicity of life. For it is not the outer affluence which prevails, but the inner abundance. The inner feelings of peace and happiness give vitality to the soul's experience. We cannot emphasize this enough, for the inner values nourish and sustain the spirit. The outer values sustain the human, who is seeking security in an insecure world. Insecure in that it is constantly changing, moving or redirecting its passage through time.

Replenishment is the momentum of creation which is continually rebuilding upon itself by replacing what has come before. It marvels in the newness of every moment reborn into its own expression, then relinquishes it unto its next successor.

The mighty power of God is constant. Its intention is to move freely according to its own Will. Many humans do not understand the Will of God which serves the Whole. It is so mighty it cannot be controlled by any individual or group. We refer to this as the flowing power of God. When human's live in the *flow*, they are allowing God's Will to guide their lives.

Have you noticed the changes, beloved ones? Have you seen God rebuilding his Earth? When you love God, there is no fear of the changes. It is the Creator's nature to provide new foundations for the growth of his new generations on Earth.

REJUVENATION

DEGREES OF LIGHT formations are now surrounding the Earth. Planet Earth is being rejuvenated and reborn, through experiencing an infusion of light particles. This effect is creating an acceleration of energies passing through the human form causing it to adapt. You may experience this sensation as a quickening or fast forward motion in your life.

It is uncertain times that you live in. Although it cannot be comprehended yet, it is very significant to the human race to occupy its space undaunted by what is occurring around you. Take up your position, and stay centered on the way of achieving that which is of the most value to your life's discoveries. We are a aware that there is fear, anger and losses. There are also new opportunities for gains and rewards.

We also know that many of you are not anxious to let go of what has been established as familiar patterns, as the old slowly makes way for the new.

The raising of Earth to Heaven is an acceleration from dark into light. You are all becoming lighter beings, like unto us who serve you from our spiritual kingdom. The acceleration of the human into its light body is part of the path of evolution for the races.

The journey into light will take you beyond your present limited sphere, into a larger dimension where the senses of form will become more acutely understood. Light expansion, beyond

84

its present known boundaries, is the direction you are all headed toward.

All of this action is preparing the way for the birth of the new generations of souls on Earth so they will have the same advantages as their forefathers. The advantages are that of self-expression, while drawing upon the Earth for means of survival.

THE RAISING OF THE SOUL TO HEAVEN

WHEN IT IS that moment when the soul is preparing to leave its flesh body a reconnoitering takes place. The soul is preparing for its journey back to the spiritual world. It starts to detach itself from its sensory perception. Often it will reflect upon its life's experiences and what it has gained or missed.

If the soul recognizes that it has not accomplished all it came to do, it will often struggle to set in motion those things which it needs to accomplish before its departure. If the outer flesh body is aged, it will present even a greater challenge to get on with the goals still remaining. The soul may put forth great strength and determination to accomplish as much as it can of its goal before giving up its body and its life on Earth.

To those who are part of the family around the soul, I would say look for the signals which are being generated by your loved one. Your loved one may not be able to communicate to you through the human level its intention or what it is about. Nevertheless, if you bypass the personality and instead tune into the soul essence, you may discover what it is struggling to do. It is good to project as much love toward the soul at this time.

The souls who have collected together and formed part of a human family share a very special bond. These souls have agreed to be part of each other's life journey. Each member of the family is sharing in a specific experience. Sometimes the human judges the experience as not good. Nevertheless, there is meaning to every action which is demonstrated.

When you become more attuned to your own soul, you will instinctively recognize that you are preparing to leave the Earth. You may feel a need to clear up loose ends, make amends with your friends or loved ones if this is the case, or become totally detached from your surroundings.

Sometimes the soul will withdraw years in advance of its leaving the Earth as it is already progressing itself or preparing itself to make the transition into the spiritual life.

In a future time era, many who are on the Earth will refrain from going through the process of long term illness or dying. The dramatic process of the dying of the flesh will be eased. The human, in this future time era, will recognize there is no need to subject itself to excessive pain and suffering of the flesh in order to leave the Earth.

I wish to speak of this now. The angels make every effort to contact the soul at the moment of its decision to depart the Earth. We wish for all of you to be in the knowing that we bathe you in the light of the Divine Father.

There is no need to be afraid when you sense our presence all around you for we project our love into your Essence. We ask, at this particular moment in your life, that you draw upon our love, coupling it deep within you and connecting to the source of our light. Some of you will be able to see us, or feel our presence around you and will immediately feel the peace which we project.

We, the angels of the light, know when you are getting ready to return to our realms for the rays around your flesh body, or your auric field changes. This is a signal unto us that you are preparing to make your transition back into spirit.

We gather around you to assist you through your transition although **we cannot lift you out of your body.** This is because of the free will which has been extended to all of God's children. Your soul must exist of its own accord.

Even in the case of the souls who must exist because their flesh body has been destroyed or taken away from them by another. We prepare the way for the soul, but we cannot interfere in what is taking place because of the free will power, or unless it is specifically asked of us.

I would emphasize again that only a small portion of your life existence is spent on the Earth. It is a wondrous place, provided by the Father to create and experience many life lessons and to grow in the knowing of these experiences.

I have spoken of your departure from the Earth, but your entrance onto the Earth is also very precious. We are always gathered around you as you depart our realms to be born onto your Earth. We send you on your way, so to speak, with our love and light to carry with you. We are, of course, saddened when we see the human veils close over you because we know you will often not remember who we are. Nevertheless, we watch over all souls while they are on Earth, and we are especially joyous when you regain your remembrance so we can share ourselves with you again.

SPIRITUAL ESSENCE

WHEN YOU PICTURE us you must realize that we are not human. We do not wear a flesh body covering our spirit as you do. Our eyes are not like yours, yet we can see. We do not have a human brain yet we can think and reason. Our body comprises particles of light formations encompassing many layers of energy. These rays of energy are multicolored like the hues in your rainbow, but much more brilliant.

Because our body is comprised of light waves it is constantly being recharged, therefore we have no need of sleep to regenerate ourself. We also have no need to eat food since our energy is automatically provided.

Whereas your Earth is a physical plane where you generate your energies from your physical bodies, the spiritual kingdom is a **mental** plane where we direct our energies through our mind. Using our mind we can create anything which pleases us to create, including the *image* **of a flesh body**, if we so choose.

We realize that you cannot see these waves of energy through your human eyes. Nevertheless, in your future discoveries, you will be able to create a form of glasses to wear over your eyes which will enable you to see the multicolored energies very clearly. In this future time era the limited world you live in will have expanded for you will be able to see beyond the range or normal capacity of the human eye.

When your delicate spirit leaves the Kingdom of God to live in the Earth's environment it must wear suitable protection. Your flesh body gives your spirit the external form it needs. Your parents create the flesh form. This enables you to leave our realms and journey to Earth to be part of the human family.

Over a period of time your flesh form becomes worn. Constant bombardment of Earth conditions plus life style, creates a breaking down and deterioration of your external body. Although your science has found ways to prolong the life of the flesh form, it cannot exist forever. Your spirit has no intention of staying on Earth for longer than it needs to be there.

When your flesh has served the purpose of its inner spirit, you will exit your flesh garment and cross over the divide again back into our domain. By concentrating upon your inner spirit and *knowing* that you return to the Kingdom of God will enable your crossing to be more simplified.

At the time of your crossing, be of the mind to get beyond the barrier back into God's realms. It will take all the energy of your spirit to push yourself across to the other side. We cannot assist in your crossing until your spirit is out of the body. The ones who have had a near death experience have felt a whooshing sound propelling them through a tunnel. The tunnel is really not a tunnel. It is your spirit **creating an opening and propelling you through the darkness of the void.** The void is that space occupied between the Earth and the Spiritual Kingdom.

Many of you who leave the Earth will mentally recreate the image of the flesh form you wore on Earth. This is because this image is still predominant in your thinking. Slowly, as the remembrance of your Earth life dims, you will begin to let go of the human image and regain your **spiritual** image, which is pure light.

When the moment comes for your departure from the Earth, you will discover that your life has not been in vain. No matter where upon the Earth you have lived, you will find comfort in the knowing that you have completed another milestone in your growth.

As you approach our realms you will be given a review of your life cycle so you may reflect on what you have gained through your experience. Remember you will not be in human form neither will you have a human brain. You will be in the knowing of your spirit. Therefore you will **see yourself through a higher vantage point with more understanding of what you traveled to Earth to achieve.**

To those on Earth who are of the thought that upon reaching our realms your life is fully complete, will discover that the learning and wisdom of growth never ceases. To remain in a state of complete fulfillment comes, not at the end of the Earth life as many presume, but after your spirit has found the ultimate answers to the ultimate knowledge it seeks.

For those who believe with all their hearts that the life of the spiritual plane is one of rest and do nothing, will find that an eternity of nothingness only produces nothing.

I have explained a little about our bodies of light and your own spirit which is also light. The information has been given to assist you to understand your inner self and to help you overcome fear.

Your beloved leader Jesus had no fear of his flesh body because he had **absolute knowledge** of his spirit.

91

SPIRIT BODY VERSUS
HUMAN BODY

THE SPIRITUAL light wave body is an essence. The flesh body is a solidified form. The spiritual world is a mental plane. The human world is a physical one.

When you look beyond your Earth you now see other galaxies. When you look beyond your human form, you will find other existences just as precious as your own. You will be looking into our realms. Our realms are as large as your Earth is small. Our people are as meaningful in our world as you are in yours. We in the spirit kingdom do not fear you, we only observe your progress toward our world.

In the spiritual kingdom, we are also learning as you are learning on your Earth plane. Slowly we progress and move into the next order. Yes, there is order here, order of progression.

We of the spiritual kingdom are not trying to overshadow our fellow beings with our individual power. We have learned better, for if we each used our power against one another in this world, we would achieve nothing.

Our bodies are made up of magnetic light waves, each wave length formation is different. The light waves of our body essence enable us to travel very quickly from one place or time span to another; we travel along the waves of current. Our body form of wave lengths exists in perfect harmony.

The portions of our weight are evenly balanced. Our bodies are perfect because we, in our present form, are fragments of the Creator's body.

Our knowledge is stored in our light waves. Our receiver, which is a form of brain, is located in the center of our essence. We receive signals from the Creator. These signals are more finely tuned than yours. We break down the signals into telepathic vibrations.

The cosmic thermo waves flow parallel to our existence. We feed on the energy to nourish our spiritual essence. We are continually being recharged through energy lifelines.

We have outgrown the human form by our learning and we now exist in the spiritual form. Our spiritual essence **is just like the essence within each of you,** except that we have experienced more learning and have progressed to where we are now.

We have explained that our bodies are made up of light waves and that our mental power can transform this energy into any shape or form which we have a mind to choose. We can take on the human form if it pleases us, we can look young or old as we see fit, or for the purpose it serves. The form we take on has **no significance,** we have learned to overcome the flesh form which is predominant in your present thinking.

We have superseded the need for a structured body because it is limiting to us and does not allow us the freedom which we now have. The structured body is cumbersome because we are aware of it and that we must carry it with us wherever we wish to go. Our light wave body allows us to penetrate solid formations. We can move up or down, backwards and forwards at will, or travel at speeds faster than the blinking of an eye.

Our light wave spiritual bodies can serve your understanding best if you consider steam vaporization. Applied heat to liquid causes vapor action to rise into the surrounding atmosphere. You cannot hold steam in your hands. It quickly reverts back to its original liquid form. This is because as the steam vapor comes into contact with a solidifying mass such as your hand, it cannot contain itself to remain in the steam structure. As with steam, our bodies of light waves cannot be **contained by a solidifying mass**. Comparing our form to yours is like water and steam. The water represents your heavy dense form, whereas our body is like the steam vaporization which rises from the water. The steam is the **same** as the water, it has only changed its form into another substance.

Our light wave spiritual body is suitable for our present life experience, which is a fullness of immeasurable quality. We are gathered together as one family. We rest peacefully because there are no threats of war upon us, no hunger or danger of extinction of any of our kind.

We live in simplicity, taking that which we need which pleases our lives. We are enhanced by each other's love and comfort; we share the Whole, but we are only a small part. But that is the beauty of our existence, we want for nothing, for we have the greatest gift of all, God's deepest love flowing through us.

SPIRITUAL KINGDOM

OUR LIFE IN the Spiritual Kingdom is very different from that of human. We are seeking to gain more knowledge and wisdom, and therefore we study principles or teachings which are impressed upon us from those closest to the Holy One. The teachings allow us to study the whole of creation for there is much to know and understand. It is like understanding the Mind of the Creator, which is so great in its magnitude, it can only be grasped in small amounts.

All of the Creator's offsprings (all of you and all of us) are fragments of the Divine Spirit. We grow through our learning capacity. In the course of our learning, we must live through many lessons in order to comprehend the meaning. Each of you on Earth are living through physical human experiences every day of your stay on the planet. These experiences are impressing degrees of learning into the consciousness of the soul. When you depart the Earth, the soul takes with it the value of the life lessons. Through these experiences it has grown larger in its understanding of all things in existence.

Many of us in the Spiritual Kingdom are in service, which means we are delegated certain responsibilities. These responsibilities are assigned according to our ability to perform. Those spiritual beings, who are more advanced in their wisdom and knowledge of the Will of God, become overseers of the planets. Others, who have mastered the physical existence on

95

Earth become teachers, assisting those souls on Earth who are eager to grow in the knowledge of what the life is about.

The Angels of the Light serve in many capacities, as God's messengers, healers, teachers, preparers of the way for the many root races. They monitor the progress of the races and report their findings back to the Godhead. Then there are the glorious Seraphim who assist the Holy Spirit. There are many councils of learned ones who meet to discuss forthcoming actions. Also numerous brotherhoods of Light, all endeavoring to perfect the future course of humanity.

Then there are the Cosmic beings, of which humanity knows little. These are the beings to whom God delegates most of his power, for they oversee the Universe. The Universe is much larger than present-day human can comprehend. The Spiritual Cosmic Beings are representatives of all the planets in your galaxy as well as the galaxies which humanity has yet to discover. There is life and spirit living upon these planets who do not have a human form. Some exist in the form of a radiance all blended together. Their learning is very different from what you are gaining on planet Earth.

All of what I have spoken of is part of God's totality. Its magnitude is far greater than can be presently explained through the human language.

The earliest teachings given to mankind were in concentrated form to help humans grow in their spiritual nature toward understanding their Godhead. Human intellectual reasoning was not developed enough in early man for him to comprehend other species of life outside his own planet, so this information was not imparted.

The challenge for the spirit fragments, who were born on

96

Earth, was to wear the flesh body form and develop it physically, mentally and spiritually. It was called self-mastery, or self-realization. Those who very quickly progressed through this challenge became masters of their own flesh body. This was a very important degree of learning for the inner spirit, for instead of being subservient to the flesh, it had conquered it.

WHITE DOVE

A WHITE DOVE approaches the Earth soon, it comes in its finest regalia to reach the sentient ones who have kept the love of the Divine Holy One within their heart and soul. The white dove I speak of is pure and divine and has been blessed with all manner of grace. Within the dove is our hopes and joys for a better understanding between the Spiritual Family and the Human Family who are our beloved brothers and sisters.

I would speak of this dove now. It is as a sign unto those on Earth who are watching that the Lord has spoken, for His virtues will be known by those in whom the dove reaches. It is a splendid revealing of our hearts unto your hearts, and it is our hope and prayers that you understand the simplicity of our communication.

It is a new beginning, a moment of glory for those who have **prepared the way for the Holy Spirit to come among you**. Prepare ye with joy for this blessed event. We call all unto the sacredness of the Holy Dove so each will find his truth in divine measure.

Let us pray that the peace and love of the Holy One be imparted in each one's heart and may this spiritual joining point the way to the destiny of the nations on Earth. We hold thee in sacredness, which is beauty in its ultimate expression.

ARCHANGEL RAPHAEL
SPEAKS ABOUT ASCENSION

ASCENSION IS THE means whereby those souls, who are of an accelerated degree of learning, can be uplifted into a sphere of more recognition of their total selves. As the ascension process comes into realization, many will become attuned to my calling.

The message has gone out to prepare thyself for the coming changes in the thoughts of humanity. We point the way unto those beings who are in the Light of the Christ, being guided by his hand and energy into a lifting motion, beyond the present scope of Earth thought. These souls will become those called by Christ to **set in motion the way heralding his return**. It will be no easy task, for the Light of the Divine One is not being received by all on Earth in its totality, but only those who are attuned to the Christ thought.

Faith is an important criteria. It is the knowing in Christ which allows Him to lift you into a greater vision of your divine spirituality.

ARCHANGEL RAPHAEL'S DECLARATION
TO HIS ANGELS ON EARTH

I dreamed of Raphael twice last night*, he seemed to be speaking to me through a cloud of beautiful pink and white mists. He held before me a printed document as if he was asking me to read something he had written. It looked very official, and I could see him name 'Raphael' printed in large letters at the top of the page.

I started to read the first few lines, not knowing its meaning. It appeared to be some kind of declaration to God and the Spiritual Kingdom.

When I awoke from my deep sleep, I quickly sat down at my desk and turned on the computer. I had this feeling that Raphael wanted me to write down the words from the document which I had seen in my dream. Closing my eyes, I could feel the energies prompting me, and I started to type without even looking at the screen . . .

According To The Law Of
RAPHAEL

The Law of my Father is a mute one, in which all are entitled to lead the fullest inquiry into the namesake of that accorded unto them in its ultimate capacity. Notwithstanding any undue discourse of inquiry which would represent an entitlement of said party or parties to that which is granted heretofore from the Divine Nature of our Sovereign Lord Almighty.

Be thou to follow unto mine thoughts in arrangement with that which holds all of the answers for advisement by me, and as me, working with my brethren in consortium for the betterment of the specie known as the Fourth Kingdom* unto the Earth sphere.

And when it has been met, to allow those souls who prefer to remain, to do so, unto their own guardianship. And those that shall reunite and return unto my flock, to lift them into a capacity of lightness whereby they might ascend unto thy Father's grace and return in triumph unto my own angels. Taking up their place as before, but with full honor bestowed upon them for their special mission unto their own knowledge.

This I set forth before you now, for approvement by the Divine Law, which supersedes all laws which are our suggestions according to the Office of Divine Spirit which has been graciously afforded to us who lead.

The way has now been made clear and mine angels are ready and prepared to sit in alignment with the Divine Plan encompassing the universal formation. So be it. I speak with my heart according to my nature of truth. Praise ye the Lord of all.

This is a documentary of Raphael, Archangel of the Lord Almighty and of his Sovereign Council of Angel Brethren. Entered and accepted.

~~~~~~~~~~~~~~~~~~~~~~~~~~~~~~~

** The human race - known in the angelic realms as the Fourth Kingdom Specie

Upon reading what I had typed, I wondered what it all meant. It appears that God has given his Archangels 'carte blanche' to perform their respective work in accordance with their Office Of Authority. Each Archangel creates their own individual laws (governing their angel followers). But the law is considered a 'suggestion' offered unto God for his final approval. This paper was an official declaration being submitted to God for Divine Acceptance.

Later on I asked Archangel Raphael what it meant and he said: "It is a declaration of the right to choose for those of my followers who are committed to serving humanity through the incarnation into flesh. It is as a message of encouragement and trust to my angel followers."

THE MONITORING OF JESUS
ON EARTH 2000 YEARS AGO

THE HOLY ONE spoke unto the people and promised them eternal life. Forasmuch as the people chose to love the Holy One, they in turn knew nothing of their Creator.

When the Holy One chose to send His Divine Messenger unto the Earth, He was opening the way for his children to speed their return unto Himself.

We observed and monitored the man Jesus of Nazareth while he was in his human form. We did not interfere with his chosen life because it was preordained that he should follow the directions of the way of salvation for the ones on Earth. We therefore observed his actions until it was time to enjoin his thoughts with those of the Divine Source of Wisdom.

This was accomplished when he was nearing the way of his ultimate teaching. His thoughts were purified of his Earth flesh and his mind was sanctioned to receive the instructions of the Holy Spirit.

The man Jesus was joined together with the Holy Spirit through brain wave communications. They were as one mind working toward the goal they sought ~ to bring love and harmony unto the Earth through the teaching of the Spiritual Essence.

The man Jesus was without a sin of the flesh. He was

of the purest body, but he was not afraid to become a part of those who had debts to repay and lessons to be learned.

He wished to enjoin his pure thoughts with his disciples, so they in turn, would learn to respect all manner of men with their meekness, which was their salvation, and became a part of their everlasting glory.

The man Jesus was glorified through his flesh suffering, but his thoughts were only for the ones he served, to point the way toward their understanding and eventual wisdom.

The Christ was filled with compassion, even unto his final breath, and sought to punish none for his pain. Because his pain was the ultimate gift that he could bestow upon his little ones, God's children.

~~~~~~~~~~~~~~~~~~~~~~~~~~~~~~~~~~~~~~

We speak of Mary, mother of Christ. She was given unto the Holy One in betrothal at an early age. She was filled with much jubilation at the promise of a son from the most high. She was most tender of thought and looked upon the coming of the Christ as the dawn of a New Age where men and women would not suffer the enslavement of their bodies and the torment of their souls.

The time came for Mary to deliver unto mankind, the child of Bethlehem and her body was made sacred to nourish the infant.

Mary became very wise and her mind was enlightened of many ways. She nourished and nurtured her infant son and marveled at his knowledge and understanding of all things.

She was given to receive the blessing, to prepare her for her son's final deliverance and she spoke to him often of her love.

She gave the tears of her heart unto the Earth's way as she beheld her son's crucifixion, and questioned not God for her deepest loss.

Mary beheld her son in his **spiritual body**, and he held her unto himself saying: '**little Mary, mother of my own heart, thee be my blessing, for I have beheld you as my mother, and no precious a gift was bestowed unto me, than the journey we shared together as one flesh.**'

Mary gave her heart unto humanity, and her heart became an everlasting part of the Earth.

ONE FOOT ON EARTH,
ONE FOOT IN HEAVEN

WE ARE PLEASED to have witnessed many endeavors by the souls on Earth to understand more about their precious spiritual essence. For these souls, a special light in the form of a blessing by me has shone forth and has coupled their present understanding with a far greater belief of what creation is all about.

Many have regained their complete spiritual recognition which has opened the door into their further development while clothed in human flesh. Mine angels are preparing to teach how to look beyond the present flesh form to help you penetrate more deeply other dimensional aspects of yourselves. Great spiritual teachers are progressing those persons who are ready to advance into more significant knowledge about human and spirit. This discovery may be a surprise to those who are locked into their special belief systems about whom they are and the spiritual kingdom of God.

We have greater faith that our brethren on Earth will move forward now beyond their present recognition of all there is to a greater totality. It is the next step beyond the infinity stage and the balancing of the male/female collective energies. The human souls must realize their greater purpose of achievement and see their own divineness. It is only through this realization that the masses can let go of their limited vision of themselves. We have

106

worked hard to advance the understanding of our existence and the spiritual kingdom. The more knowledge you have, the more you will understand that we are all one family in spirit.

Afterthoughts

Something to Consider

THERE ARE MORE aspects to be learned about spirit than we can ever realize. It is a gift for us to be able to understand that we are more than just a complex form. A flesh body supplies us with the means to sample the human existence for a limited number of years, before it starts the process of deterioration and finally dies. The unknown probability of what awaits us after this occurrence does not always satisfy our curiosity. In order to comprehend more about our evolution, we need to uncover the hidden facets of our spiritual roots and divine heritage.

The task set before us is no small fete. It requires a willingness to take a giant leap forward unaided, for no one else can do it for us. Searching deeply for more answers to our spiritual origin is the first step toward discovery. Once we arrive at this point of determination, the fullness of our inner self starts to unfold.

In our present era, we are being encouraged more than ever by the Angelic Brethren. These spiritual hosts are showing to the masses that there are other dimensions of existence and far more knowledge to be explored than ever before. But are we ready to take this step forward to bridge the void between our human life and our spiritual life?

It is only a small step from human to spirit, but we may have hesitated far too long because of the uncertainty of what lies beyond. It takes courage and determination to move into unexplored territory, but no matter what our fellow beings may choose to do, the individual choice is still ours.

The challenge we face is returning to the pioneer stage of exploration, for unless we are willing to venture forth, we will stay on the merry-go-round forever.

There are those Heavenly Hosts who have been preparing for this special time, as it is an era of inquiry. Our mind intellect has approached a phase of greater comprehension about what its life's meaning serves. Perhaps it may come as a shock that the Earth existence is one of the greatest challenges the soul faces. When our soul is born into the Earth environment, it is ready to step into combat and battle the trials and errors of the human existence. For as long as it takes to become comfortable in the human body, there is a turning point in which the soul must start to extract itself from its human traits to seek out the original source of its origin.

It is all part of the learning, to be able to live in our human environment with no remembrance of our spiritual core. Gradually the human starts to conquer the veils of separation to reunite itself with its memory of spirit. At this degree of understanding, our human part and soul part are no longer separate, for an integration or blending starts to occur. This allows for a far better evaluation of our life, for our human intellect is now **aware** of the existence of its own soul's purpose and allows the soul to override its mental conditioning.

Our soul has now moved from backseat driver, to taking control and steering the whole human body flesh. We are now able to see with the eyes of the soul, thus creating a very different life perspective. From this moment forth we become a total of ourself, our human and soul working together as one unit, instead of as a duality. Thereby utilizing the human expression to its fullest value without fear, knowing that the life continues onward, even after the physical body flesh becomes unusable.

There are many among us who are now ready to take this quantum leap in consciousness, which is referred to as ascension. We are ascending from spirit, through matter, back to spirit in **conscious** understanding of what we're about. When we pass through the portal of ascension, it means we have finally graduated cum laude from this plane of existence.

Experiencing the Father's Love

To read all about God and his love in a book is one thing, to **experience the flowing spirit** of God is another. As a child I was part of a church, attended Sunday school and sang in the choir. I read all about God in the scriptures but I never felt that close. He was in heaven and I was on Earth.

When the Holy One touched my life, my whole concept changed. I felt **His Nature flowing through me.** This flowing of infinite love was delicately sensitive, all compassionate and understanding, gentle and kind. All of this and much more was conveyed **in the feeling** which flowed through me. Everything about the Holy Father's love **is conveyed in the feeling.** I cannot emphasize this enough. When God touches you, every impression or concept about Him you have ever formed, changes. His energy feels joyous, happy, non-conforming, free. You experience bliss in the ultimate.

In that moment, He conveyed to me in His loving energy that He is a caring Father. This was a very different God I had read about in the scriptures or was taught to worship on my knees. He was reaching out to me on my level, and I experienced the deepest feeling that He, as a Father adores us, his spiritual children. Something deep within me recognized we could be doing **a terrible injustice** to our Spiritual Father by thinking that our soul is **separate from Him,** as this thought sets up a **block** between Father and child.

111

All at once I began to see that I had compared God to my human body image instead of my **spiritual image**. If we could go beyond seeing God through our human eyes, and instead envision God with our spiritual eyes, then perhaps we would get a very different concept of our Creator. I think He is too large to fit into the dimensions of a human frame. Or even fit into a throne room for that matter!

God has indicated in his messages, that he created us out of his own body of spirit. After I digested this suggestion, it made sense. We are all created out of the same spiritual substance. What else would God use to make **his children** other than his own Spiritual Essence?

The Archangel has already indicated that the power of God's body is the life line (or Life force) of the universe. We know there is an energy or power which is part of everything in creation.

So I asked the Archangel how God created us out of his body. Raphael replied that God divided part of His Spiritual Essence from the rest of his Spiritual body. The part which was divided became unjoined from the Whole of Spirit. This same spiritual part unjoined from the Whole of God's body, was given a life of its own. That is it was given its own free will to explore and discover. We are still God's children, being a part of his own Spiritual Body, but only a **fragment** of the Whole.

We are spiritual fragments of the Whole of God, that is why He said we were created in his **spiritual likeness**. This is the reason God gives his spiritual children the title of divine. He looks upon us as a reflection of himself, his own beauty. He watches our movement through time and is delighted at our discoveries. God's need is that we do not forget that we carry part of his love inside of us, our inner spirit.

It seems there will come a moment when our spiritual essence will return to God and re-merge with our Father's body again. This is when we have had our fill of traveling the Earth and exploring the universe. What we take back to the Father with us as our offering, is the knowledge we have gained from our life experiences.

We cannot re-merge with God's Essence until we have become purified. We must be purified so we do not contaminate the Whole. This purification comes through the flame. In the past, humanity has mistakenly misinterpreted the word 'flame' to mean fire. The **spiritual flame** consumes all the impurities which the soul has collected from its experiences. It is not the same as the human fire, or burning of the flesh. The spiritual flame can only be used in the hands of those specially trained to perform this service. This cleansing is performed on the **spirit when it is not in its flesh body**. The object is not to destroy or burn the flesh, but to cleanse the spirit.

In one of his messages, the Holy One has said that all **spirit must eventually return from whence it came**. Perhaps this may take another billion years or more, no one knows the exact time, only the Father.

ARE WE GIVING OUR SOUL
ENOUGH ATTENTION?

IF THE HUMAN body and brain receives its nourishment only from its Earth surroundings, then the soul inside becomes undernourished. It cries out for spiritual food for development. If it is denied its daily ration of 'living water' it will sink into despondency and even a silent death in the body, while the flesh and brain continue through the motions of existing.

Therefore, the two parts, flesh and soul must relate to each other and harmonize together. In this way, the true meaning of the Earth life can be fulfilled. We can help our soul by applying suitable intellect and judgment in our daily choices. The human logic and inner soul **should never conflict** with each other, for in doing so, disharmony or disease ensues.

When our innermost feelings are not pursued because our brain is relying upon our social conditioning and logic to make its decisions and advancements, then our soul becomes unhappy. We are cutting of its lifeline for it cannot get through the brain's programed memory long enough to be heard. In desperation, our soul sometimes will resort to extremes to get us to stop and listen to its cries. "I am part of you" it says, "I need to be heard too."

Often, our inner soul will send its call for help through our dreams, while the brain is resting and cannot interfere. The soul uses symbols* taken from a person's life pattern to send its messages through the consciousness of the brain. These communications come in the form of pictures. The scene it plays is a message of something it needs to demonstrate for us to be aware of. It directs its communication through the subconscious to the conscious human waking state.

Sometimes the message is 'feed me', but our brain often misinterprets and feeds the human flesh body instead. The flesh body receives overindulgence, while the starving spirit continues to cry out for inner nourishment.

Our inner child (soul) often becomes trapped by habitual thought-patterning, i.e., we do the same thing every day, out of our conditioned mind set. The soul which is alive in us continually needs **new experiences** to grow through and learn from.

~~~~~~~~~~~~~~~~~~~~~~

* the language of the spirit is symbols.

SPIRITUAL BLUEPRINT

HOW MANY OF us would think of traveling across country without some kind of road map? The same strategy applies to our soul. When we leave our spiritual home and are born into the flesh, we have a definite purpose in mind. We carry with us, encoded in our soul memory, a **blueprint** for achieving our goals. It is like a road map for us to follow with all the details set up in the ethereal. When we pay attention to our intuition, we'll instinctively know when to make a right or left turn, or if its time to change direction, so we can link up and achieve the desired results.

By being out of tune with our soul we are driving through our life blindly, not knowing if the way we are heading is the right one for us. Taking control of our life means remembering what we came to do and getting on with it.

Our blueprint is also a timetable, and we certainly want to be on time so we don't miss our soul connections. This is called cross-linking, it means we deliberately cross another's path so we can link up with that person. For the maximum results, everything is perfectly timed, ready to be set in motion by us.

Our ethereal blueprint contains the proposed route to take to achieve our soul goals. Our definite purpose for being born on Earth is projected in the ethereal pattern. This is not set in concrete but only **projected.** This means when we get to Earth, we can modify or change the course of our destiny if we so

116

choose. However, once an event occurs and we physically live through it, it becomes history. We cannot change or turn the clock backward. That is why it is good to check our blueprint for the future, to be sure we're taking those actions which benefit our soul.

In order for us to be in the right place at the right time is going to take some serious consideration. After all, we don't want to be caught up in someone else's circumstances that we have no need to experience.

It is like looking at a colored dot matrix, each dot represents a specific goal our soul wishes to accomplish. Some of the dots are larger than others, this infers a very important milestone our soul desires to achieve. The colors are coded according to our soul ray* identity. Also they are synchronized, which means we must accomplish our first goal before moving toward our second, etc.

If we could see this blueprint through our human eyes, we would see a definite pattern of formation. It would show us the time span we have allowed our self to move through a specific life lesson, before moving onto the next experience. The more we 'tune in' and understand this soul strategy sufficiently, the easier it will become for us to maneuver our self into the place that's right for us, as well as put forth the energy to create the type of work we need to be involved in.

~~~~~~~~~~~~~~~~~~~~~~~~~~~~~

* In one of his messages Archangel Raphael speaks about the vibrant colored energies which comprise our ethereal body. These rays of energy serve a specific purpose. Raphael, for example, uses the green ray because of the healing properties. Archangel Michael uses the blue energy ray to transmute negative energies. The lavender energy is used in religious benefit because of its high spiritual content.

~~~~~~~~~~~~~~~~~~~~~~~~~~~~

The Spiritual Child

The very young child is more aware of its spiritual nature, it automatically speaks its truth and behaves in a very natural way. Often it tries to communicate in signs and pictures which is the language of the spirit.

Gradually, as the spiritual child becomes bombarded with human teachings, which it absorbs from its surroundings, it loses its natural innocence and becomes molded into society's conditioning. It may take years (perhaps never), to reawaken to its spiritual memory.

As parents, if we choose to encourage the infant to remember its spiritual purpose before the young brain is molded into the way of society, the thought would stimulate the infant's inner memory and shift the child more into its spiritual alignment.

Our spirit speaks a very different language from our human. It is symbolic and therefore, we need to learn to interpret the impressions coming from our inner instincts and intuitions and follow through on them.

My Spirit

I Come From a Place Wherein there is no time ~

A Sacred Scroll unravels to reveal

The elements of my succession.

Through the template of my journey

I am a Being without a home,

For I travel the intricacies of life's

adventures ~

A never-ending road, full of surprises!

But when I go, I am not

forgotten

For there is always a flicker of

Light

That remains, ever-glowing

Its radiance illuminating

The Now

Of my existence

Order Form

Rev. H. McClellan
Stuart Victor Publishing
P.O. Box 60322, Phoenix, Arizona 85082-0322

Please send the following:

■   God Speaks His Heart $15.95

Name:_____

Address_____

City_____ State_____Zip_____

Telephone_____

■   Also available a limited supply of 8 x 10 colored photos of Archangel Raphael copied from His portrait. $15.00 each, plus tax and postage.

■   "My Spirit" poem is available 8 x 10 suitable for Framing.

■   The Archangel Raphael doll will be designed by a doll artist in the near future. With Raphael's permission this replica is being created to bring the children closer to the real angels.   Write for information.

Sales Tax
Please add **7.15%** for books, photos, poem sent to Arizona addresses.

Shipping & Handling:
Book/ Photo/Poem add **$2.00** regular mail, extra copies add **$1.00** .   Book UPS **$3.50**

Product may be returned if not satisfied

Order Form

Rev. H. McClellan
Stuart Victor Publishing
P.O. Box 60322, Phoenix, Arizona 85082-0322

Please send the following:

■   God Speaks His Heart $15.95

Name:_____

Address_____

City_____ State_____Zip_____

Telephone_____

■   Also available a limited supply of 8 x 10 colored photos of Archangel Raphael copied from His portrait. $15.00 each, plus tax and postage.

■   "My Spirit" poem is available 8 x 10 suitable for Framing.

■   The Archangel Raphael doll will be designed by a doll artist in the near future. With Raphael's permission this replica is being created to bring the children closer to the real angels. Write for information.

Sales Tax
Please add **7.15%** for books, photos, poem sent to Arizona addresses.

Shipping & Handling:
Book/ Photo/Poem add **$2.00** regular mail, extra copies add **$1.00** . Book UPS **$3.50**

Product may be returned if not satisfied

Order Form

Rev. H. McClellan
Stuart Victor Publishing
P.O. Box 60322, Phoenix, Arizona 85082-0322

Please send the following:

■   God Speaks His Heart $15.95

Name:_____

Address_____

City_____ State_____Zip_____

Telephone_____

■   Also available a limited supply of 8 x 10 colored photos of Archangel Raphael copied from His portrait. $15.00 each, plus tax and postage.

■   "My Spirit" poem is available 8 x 10 suitable for Framing.

■   The Archangel Raphael doll will be designed by a doll artist in the near future. With Raphael's permission this replica is being created to bring the children closer to the real angels. Write for information.

Sales Tax
Please add **7.15%** for books, photos, poem sent to Arizona addresses.

Shipping & Handling:
Book/ Photo/Poem add **$2.00** regular mail, extra copies add **$1.00** . Book UPS **$3.50**

Product may be returned if not satisfied